EASTERN HEROES
THE CLONES OF BRUCE LEE

SPECIAL EDITION

Published by

Rick Baker

Ken Miller

Printed by

All rights reserved. No part of this publication may be reproduced or transmitted by any means, graphic, electronic or mechanical, including photocopying, recording, taping or any information storage and retrieval system, without prior written permission of the publishers.
Copyright Eastern Heroes.

All photos & pictures © the copyright owners.

CONTENTS

06 - THE MEN WHO MADE BRUCEPLOITATION SUPERCOOL
David Gregory, **Michael Worth** and **Frank Djeng** talk about their amazing documentary *Enter the Clones of Bruce*.

18 - BRUCE LI PROFILE
Ken Miller provides the lowdown on the Bruce clone who is definitely one of the most popular of the imitators with the fans.

20 - BRUCE LE PROFILE
Ken Miller fills you in on what you need to know about Bruce Le, and Rick Baker provides a cool anecdote!

24 - DRAGON LEE PROFILE
Rick Baker explains what made Dragon Lee such an entertaining kung fu actor and Bruceploitation star.

26 - BRUCE LIANG PROFILE
Ken Miller reveals how Bruce Liang's rough childhood helped him to become such a tough cookie and awesome on-screen fighter.

28 - ART ATTACK!
Neal Adams was one of the greatest comic book artists ever. He also created amazing film posters, and some were for Bruceploitation flicks!

38 - BRUCEPLOITATION MOVIE REVIEWS
Ken Miller and Rick Baker review LOADS and LOADS of action-packed, madness-filled, colourful Bruceploitation films!

82 - SAMMO HUNG - THE BEST BRUCE MIMIC!
Rick Baker contends that Sammo Hung, the big-boned master of top-notch movie action, is, in fact, the best Bruce Lee imitator there is.

86 - THE BLACK DRAGON
A chat with **Ron Van Clief**, the star of such entertaining Bruceploitation films as *Kung Fu Fever* and *The Black Dragon's Revenge*.

98 - BRUCEPLOITATION POSTER GALLERY
Drool over some ace Bruceploitation film posters, shared with us by **David Gregory** and **Michael Worth**.

David Gregory clone drawing by Russell Fox

Cover Illustration and clones drawings by Darren Wheeling

Ron Van Clief drawings by Zilla Man

BRUCE LE

BRUCEPLOITATION

In this Special Edition we dive into the world of Bruceploitation. A sub-genre born in the aftermath of Bruce Lee's death, it was very much part of the cool milieu of the period, which was awash with Blaxploitation flicks, kung fu comics and funky film scores. But Bruceploitation films faced criticism from dedicated enthusiasts who saw these substitute Lees simply as poor imitations - actors who lacked the authenticity of the martial arts icon and who appeared in films that exploited Lee's legacy. Despite this initial backlash, the last two decades have witnessed a transformative shift. Bloggers, websites and social media platforms have helped with the reevaluation of Bruceploitation, fostering a resurgence in popularity and cultivating a fervent cult following amongst martial arts movie fans.

A new generation of enthusiasts now celebrate these once-dismissed low budget, often madcap films and the actors who embodied Bruce Lee's spirit, recognising the unique charm, the cheesiness, the exciting action and the uninhibited entertainment value that these Bruceploitation movies bring.

And this cult-tastic sub-genre is getting a major boost now, thanks to the release of the captivating, energetic Severin Films documentary *Enter the Clones of Bruce*, and the accompanying Bruceploitation Blu-ray box set, which has been titled... 'The Game of Clones'! Ha! Awesome!

There's a huge Bruceploitation film reviews section to look out for in this issue (including reviews for many of the movies featured in The Game of Clones box set), plus interviews with the makers behind the *Enter The Clones of Bruce* doc, and there are also profiles of Bruce Li, Bruce Le, Dragon Lee and Bruce Liang: the Bruce Lee clones who all appear in *Enter the Clones of Bruce*. A look at the truly amazing kung fu-themed illustration work of comic book legend Neal Adams, a gallery of eye-catching Bruceploitation film posters, Darren Wheeling's utterly superb clones illustrations and much more lie in wait for you.

And if that wasn't enough, check out page 76 for details on how you can get 5% off The Game of Clones box set! Yay!

Ken Miller & Rick Baker
Editors

BRUCEPLOITATION

Etymology
Bruce ("Bruce Lee") + *-sploitation*

Noun
(film, martial arts) a genre of exploitation film that exploits the legacy of Bruce Lee through copycats.
(Definition of 'Bruceploitation' on Wiktionary)

DRAGON LEE

Design and Layout
Ken Miller

Contributors
Simon Pritchard, Rick Baker, Darren Wheeling, Russell Fox, Zilla Man

Special Thanks
David Gregory, Frank Djeng, Michael Worth, Ron Van Clief, Toby Russell, Severin Films

BRUCEPLOITATION

The hugely enjoyable Bruceploitation documentary *Enter the Clones of Bruce* received a lot of great reviews and positive feedback during its tour of the film festival circuit last year.

Shortly after a screening at London's FrightFest, Simon Pritchard and Rick Baker interviewed David Gregory, the director and executive producer of *Clones*, along with producer Michael Worth, who also appears in the movie as one of the on-screen commenters, and producer Frank Djeng, who arranged all the filming in Hong Kong, Thailand and South Korea.

RB: I was there at the beginning of the Bruceploitation boom when I was in the queue to be turned away from *Enter the Dragon* in '73. I remember the aftermath when films like *The True Game of Death* and others were released. People were so naive they thought they would see a Bruce Lee film. That's how it was in those days, the posters depicted a Bruce Lee image. I think through the internet, in the last twenty years or so, that Bruceploitation has really come into its own. Now there's a new physical media collectors market, do you find it's a great help with a documentary like this?

DG: That's certainly what makes it worthwhile for us on a financial level when we do one of these substantial documentaries. We can then release the physical edition of it. During this process we've been picking up the rights to a bunch of Bruceploitation films, desperately trying to find usable film elements to scan them and restore them - but that's a whole different matter!

It's a huge problem because basically the negatives are gone and there's not one where we found the original reel. Actually, that's not true, for *The Dragon Lives Again* we found the original camera negative, but it was in such bad condition that when they tried to pull it off, it was so sticky it just broke, so basically *The Dragon Lives Again* is still sitting in the Hong Kong Film Archive. It will sit there so hopefully at some point in the future, when the technology has improved, it can be remastered.

Until that point, we've had to use the internegative, which is basically cropped and was also struck from a print, it wasn't struck from the negative. Then there's the American Genre Film Archives - there's an American release print of *The Dragon Lives Again*, which is actually in surprisingly good condition. And as you know, a lot of these movies, which were released theatrically, those prints have just not survived.

RB: When HD came out and Letterbox, I did all the acquisition buying for the labels Hong Kong Legends and Made in Hong Kong. When we went to Hong Kong, we found some of these negatives in old barns: that's how we found *Drunken Master*. At the time DVD was just coming out and it was a new thing. But the amount of mould on them and having to go through the footage frame by frame back then in 2001 was horrific. It became a labour of love for these films, as most companies wouldn't bother wasting their time and money on such a task.

DG: There are so many horror stories like that for the films we have restored for my label, Severin Films, but Bruceploitation negatives are the worst that I have seen in terms of an entire sub-genre of films. Trying to find usable elements has been a bit of an uphill battle, but we've managed to find some prints that are in good enough condition to scan, restore and pull the colour out of them, even if they're faded.

Are those nunchucks under your sheet, or are you just happy to see us?

We've been able to pull the colour out with digital techniques.

We will be releasing more than one volume of Bruceploitation films, along with the documentary in early 2024.

RB: Michael, I know this has been a long journey, six years in the making. What did it feel like to see this documentary come to fruition and on the big screen?

MW: It's kind of hard to put into words because there's so much going on at once for me personally on a number of levels. One is just being able to get the certain information I had on Bruceploitation on-screen, but also the information that I and nobody else had ever heard, by going directly to the 'horse's mouth', getting these people for the documentary.

As David was just saying, this sub-genre was like the worst in terms of finding elements: trying to find scripts, trying to find even original posters, and sometimes trying to find almost anything on this!

Bruceploitation was such an ephemeral idea in many ways. As we all know, when it came out at the time it was like, "Yeah, it's going to play for a few weeks in America. A few weeks in Europe, a few weeks in Hong Kong,

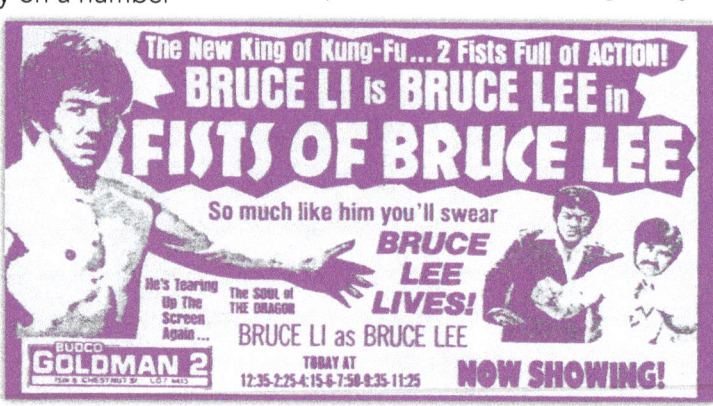

wherever, and then it's gone." And that's, of course, why we're also not finding prints and negatives, because they were also actually using the prints, the original prints, to cut up for stills for the posters.

There are a lot of emotional yet satisfying aspects to this for me: watching and learning this process,

The *Enter the Clones of Bruce* documentary was premiered on June 10th 2023 at the Tribeca Festival

and then with David, Frank and Jim, our camera guy, going out to Hong Kong and Taiwan and South Korea, sitting with these people and engaging with them, sometimes getting information, sometimes just watching them talk or laugh, or in some cases for us, seeing them on their last few months on Earth.

David did such a great job with this documentary. I can't say it enough. He's compiled the information in an informative way that shows not just the silliness of it, the strangeness of it, but also the emotional side where a lot of these people are making these films and getting work from it, also doing it in an entertaining way. You don't have to know Bruce Lee. You don't have to even know Bruceploitation to come into this movie and enjoy it.

Now, just to end this, I want to repeat what David was just alluding to: there's a whole other aspect to this project, which is the recovering, restoration and discovery of these movies themselves. We talked about it in the documentary, you get enough overview, you get to see some elements, and maybe a new appreciation for it. But now it's time to really start putting these films out properly, making the best versions we can, that will be available for people to see, hopefully forever.

SP: David, what influenced you to make a documentary about Bruceploitation and how did it start?

DG: This whole thing started pretty much the day that I met Frank and Michael, when we were doing this audio commentary with Ric Myers for *Films of Fury* and the penny dropped. When I first talked to Michael after the first audio recording I was like, yeah, who were these Bruceploitation guys? I always wondered. I learned pretty soon after seeing *Enter the Dragon* and going to the video shop and saying, "I want to see more of these movies." When I got them I thought, "Umm, these guys aren't actually Bruce Lee." I think it was when I saw *Fist of Fear, Touch of Death* (1980) and realised that Bruce Lee was not in that movie, other than that on-camera interview that's dodgy anyway, the way it was dubbed. Anyway, anything from the low-budget trenches of the exploitation realm always fascinates me. This is one

Italian poster artwork for *Bruce Lee: The Man, the Myth* (1976)

area I wanted to know more about. So I talked to Michael about it, and of course brought Frank on. Frank is essential because he basically was able to make the connection in Hong Kong to actually start this thing for real. You know I have not shot in Hong Kong before, I certainly hadn't been to Thailand or South Korea, so these are all things you need a producer to make these things happen, and that's where Frank and Vivian came in.

SP: Michael, the film explores Bruce Lee and the cultural impact of his death, and how Bruce was used to promote these Bruceploitation films.

MW: You went in every time hoping to see a clip or something, or maybe see something that wasn't already understood. Sometimes you knew that Bruce Lee was going to be nowhere near the particular movie, but you wanted to go see Shih Kien from *Enter the Dragon* or Bolo, or whomever it might be from one of the movies that you associate with Bruce Lee, and that would even pull people in.

It was a crazy time because the West was using every opportunity to Bruce-ify these kung fu movies, some of which had zero to do with Bruce Lee. Some of my favourite posters that I own are films like *Green Dragon Inn*. It has a great cover, you know, and it was also released as *Bruce is Loose*. That kind of marketing in the United States was so prevalent when I was growing up that you would always see some brief drawing of Bruce in the background to these posters but it had nothing to do with him! And so that's why I'm interested in it.

What I think is true of a lot of genres is that these films were hated for a while. I have a podcast called *The Clones Cast* and the tagline I wrote for this refers to Bruceploitation as 'the red-headed stepchild of the kung fu genre'. People thought these films were so dumb, but we're entering another phase now where people are actually loving them because we have now stepped away from the time they were trying to deceive the audience, and we can now look at them for what

they were and the representation they gave Bruce at the time.

SP: Some of the advertising got pretty low, though, showing footage from Bruce's funeral, his coffin on a poster...

MW: Yes, within the documentary David covers these posters, including Ron Van Clief's *The Black Dragon's Revenge* (aka *The Death of Bruce Lee*, also known in the UK as *The Black Dragon Revenges the Death of Bruce Lee*), which actually has a picture of Bruce Lee dead on the poster. This image was removed from subsequent posters very quickly.

SP: What direction do you think Bruce Lee's films would have taken if he had the opportunity and is there any truth that he was planning on starring in *Stoner* (1974)?

MW: Bruce Lee was going to do a film called *A Man Called Tiger* with Jimmy Wang Yu and had this falling out with Lo Wei, so he then went off and made *Way of the Dragon*. Of course Bruce went right into *Game of Death*. *Game of Death* became kind of filler time for Bruce and he had weeks and weeks on set whilst he was trying to see if *Enter the Dragon* was happening or whether they were going to go a different way. By the time *Enter the Dragon* was done, Bruce wasn't thinking so much about *Game of Death*: he had that Shaw Brothers screen test, so that was a consideration, and Bruce also loved James Bond and was talking about a film with George Lazenby, but it was not *Stoner*.

SP: Frank, how did you get into kung fu films?

FD: I grew up watching these films on TV and I'd see the commercials of the new ones coming out in theatres like *Crippled Avengers*, and *36 Chambers of Shaolin*. I thought I'd try and go see them and the guy at the door would say I'm too young to get in, so that just made me more curious. When I got a chance to go see these movies, I would, or I would take my dad to see them. We saw *Spiritual Kung Fu*, *Young Master*, those sorts of films.

Then, when *Fist of Fury* was first re-released in the theatres in 1980, I went to see it in private and that was my first exposure to Bruce Lee, as prior to that you could not see any Bruce Lee movies, they wouldn't show them on TV and that's how it started my love for seeing these films.

DG: We had actually been connected long before the documentary, it must have been on IMDb at first or something like that.

FD: Working with Eureka actually started after the idea for the documentary was conceived. Eureka contacted me and asked if they could use my work for the liner notes and I said, "Fine." They then asked whether I wanted to do any audio commentary for them as they were doing a Sammo Hung box set. Mike Leeder had committed to doing the commentary on two of the three films and they asked me if I would like to do *Iron Fisted Monk* and I said, "Sure!" I thought I had done a terrible job - I had done audio commentary before, but that was a long time ago, but they liked it and said, "Would you like to do more?" and that's how I got started.

SP: You also did the commentary for Arrow Video's *Bruce Lee at Golden Harvest* 4K Ultra HD box set. How did that come to fruition?

FD: Arrow reached out to me and said they were working on this Bruce Lee set and they would like to do some special features that are unique and will be different from all the other extra features you see on other Bruce Lee releases. I said you have to talk to Michael, as I think Michael has a unique way of visualising the thing you are trying to show and he'll be a worthwhile addition to whatever features you want. Michael ended up doing two features for them as mini-documentaries for the Bruce Lee

SP: How did you get into the film industry, you have become quite the voice in the UK for the special features on the Blu-ray releases?

FD: You have David to thank for that! David was the one who introduced me to Eureka Entertainment. Eureka had been looking for me for quite some time. They were releasing *Last Hurrah for Chivalry* and they wanted to reprint the liner notes I wrote for it. For whatever reason, they could not find me and they reached out to David, who introduced me.

set and in terms of audio commentary we needed to get him in for the films.

We also did the audio commentaries for both *Way of the Dragon* and *Tower of Death* (aka *Game of Death II*).

We hoped to do more as Michael is a cinematographer so has a lot of experience in talking about how the visuals are done, the camera angles, the use of lighting, and all that stuff which really added to people's understanding of the film as an artistic piece of work, and that's what I want to do with my commentaries.

I am hoping that Michael and I have both helped in some way to contribute to people's understanding of Bruce Lee and the artistic values of his films.

SP: Are there any commentaries you are currently working on that you can tell us about?

FD: It is mainly Stephen Chow and Jet Li films coming out soon.

I have just done *From Beijing With Love* and I'm doing the two *Royal Tramp* films this week. *Dr. Wai in The Scripture with No Words* is coming and, yes, there'll be more.

SP: Michael, you have two books coming out, *Martial Art: A History of Bruceploitation Posters* and *You Must Be Tired of Living - A Filmmaker's Life*

If they really wanted to make the grade, clone actors needed to wear some big sunglasses and get their hair cut that very special Bruce Lee way!

Challenge of the Tiger (1980)

Journey Through Bruceploitation. Can you tell us about them, please?

MW: The book with the original posters in it is done and we're just finalising it.

If you go to https://bruceploitation.net/ you will see a 'work-in-progress' website where you can check these out. They are not up for sale yet. I'm trying to time the release of the poster book with the rest of the festivals David is attending to complement the promotion of the documentary.

The other book, it feels like I have been working on for half my life, the one that will be the exhaustive 'bible' about the whole subject. I'm going to try and tie-in the release of that with the documentary on home video. David, Frank and I are trying to time everything together. It's going well and I'm really excited about it.

This is such a moment to do this. It wasn't necessarily planned but this is like the year of the rebirth of Bruceploitation. So it's so ideal that this is when we begin this onslaught of putting material out on these films, bringing these films back and it's a labour of love. We talked about David and his documentary, but one thing you must remember is the amount of finger-crossing and money David has had to put in trying to track down, restore these movies and do a good job.

The thing about Severin products is it's not just a film released with a bonus trailer on DVD. David will try to find more audio, will think, "What else can we do to add to the context of the film for the audience?"

So this year, with the books, the movies, and the events, I am still walking on cloud nine with this.

SP: David, what special features are you expecting to add to the home video release of the *Enter the Clones of Bruce* documentary?

DG: We filmed at a bunch of specific locations that were from the actual Bruce Lee films. Frank did a piece to the camera about all these different places in the documentary but it will

SOME OF THE INTERVIEWEES AND COMMENTERS FEATURED IN *ENTER THE CLONES OF BRUCE...*

Bruce Li • Bruce Le • Dragon Lee • Bruce Liang • Angela Mao • Phillip Ko • Godfrey Ho • Yasuaki Kurata • Michael Worth • Sammo Hung • Lo Meng • Eric Tsang

The Clones of Bruce Lee (1980) is the film that inspired the title of the documentary

be its own featurette on one of the discs. Same for all the outtakes where the interviewees talk about working with Bruce Lee or meeting Bruce Lee, in a lot of cases. So there will be a lot more context to the documentary and Michael is spearheading this, so there will be a wealth of information.

SP: Did you get to see around the old Shaw Brothers Studios?

MW: Well yeah, Jim, the camera guy and I got in a lot of trouble.

DG: Yes, they went creeping about the sets and we got the shots but I'm glad we did it! Frank was shouting, "We're not allowed over here! Quick, we gotta get out of here!" as we ran off.

FD: That was funny, that was when the late Mona Fong (Run Run's wife) saw us wandering around basically trespassing on the Shaw lot all the way from her office on the top floor. She called down to security, asking who these guys were and why they were there. Then we were told we had five minutes to get out of there.

DG: But we did get what we wanted, and did apologise later. It was cool there, especially when I got the footage from the shooting of The

Legend of the Seven Golden Vampires, which we used briefly at the beginning of the documentary. I just imagined what it would have been like to see the studio hustling and bustling and full of action, but what we saw of course was this crumbling relic of what it used to be.

MW: When Frank and I were out looking for the locations, and we went to one of the places people don't talk too much about, and I was standing there and my brain was exploding as I realised that we were at the Golden

Dragon Lee in Enter Three Dragons

Harvest studio. The obvious places to visit, which we did, were in Macau and 'Pigeon Park', where Bruce kicks the sign off the wall. Frank also went back to see where they filmed some of the *Enter the Dragon* scenes.

There was this time I was sitting there on Old Hammer Road with Frank and

French poster for *Goodbye Bruce Lee: His Last Game of Death* (1975)

Vivian, going, "This is where Bruce fought Chuck Norris or this is where he fought Kareem Abdul-Jabbar, this is where he fought Bob Baker", and it was surreal that all these iconic action scenes were filmed right where we were. It was the same when we were at Shaw Brothers, thinking about the movies that had been filmed there: *Mad Monkey Kung Fu*, *Invincible Shaolin*, you know, everything that was filmed there, the people that walked through that door.

SP: David, did this whet your appetite to make/release more kung fu films?

DG: Of course!

We've even had to get a couple of films that aren't Bruceploitation films in order to do the deal for the documentary. We have considerably more potential for sure.

SP: What are your plans for the documentary and what special editions do you have in mind?

DG: At the moment, we have approximately twenty festival spots around the world, so it will have its life around the festivals first. Meanwhile, we are still compiling a box set of Bruceploitation films containing around ten films. We are currently deciding which films should go into Box One. We settled on a pre-concrete lineup. Michael and I are now working out what the extras for these films will be, which he will primarily produce.

MW: These extras are not going to be 'fluff'. We're really taking our time to work out what people want to see, and what is available. There is so much footage we shot during the documentary that we have of the actors and the films, we're going all-out with these releases.

SP: The difference here, I think, is with Hollywood special features, I can find out about a film independently of the special features due to the wealth of

Bruce Le's Greatest Revenge (1979)

a more subjective perspective.

DG: Yes, it was about getting that balance where it can't just be for the people that already know a lot about this type of cinema. Simon, I remember you were very complimentary about the film after seeing it, and it is important that people like you are pleased as well, as we're getting these in-depth talks with interviewees who might have not been interviewed in this context before, for this kind of project. But, also, *Clones* has this preamble to it (all about Bruce Lee) because you'd be surprised about the amount of people who don't know that much detail about Bruce Lee.

David at the L'Étrange Festival for the Clones French premiere

FD: I agree, you need to strike that balance between introducing a subject matter to people who have never seen this genre and also pleasing the fans who have known these films all along, so as not to offend them by telling them all the stuff they already know. So I think this documentary really strikes a good balance and we're not just pandering to general audiences with our approach to the subject matter. This is a documentary for newcomers and for long-time fans of this genre, so both sides will feel the documentary was made for them. Thank you.

SP: Thank you all again

---

information out there. With these more niche/cult films, the special features on these discs are often the only place for fans to learn more about their favourite films. What are your thoughts?

DG: Quality special features are very important to me. They can't just be any old rubbish. These are small productions in their own right and they need to be good and include the right people. That's why both Frank and Michael will be involved with a lot of other important people who actually know the subject for this project.

MW: One fun fact: the cost of some of the special features is more than it costs to make the actual films!

SP: Thank you all for your time. Is there anything else you would like to add?

DG: I appreciate being able to have people like Frank and Michael along on this ride with me as this is the first documentary feature I've done where my knowledge was only superficial when we started. I obviously knew about Bruceploitation and had seen various films, but I didn't know anything about the life or history of the four main Bruces we got to talk to and the filmmakers behind it.

To me, this was an exploration where I wanted to learn more and, if I do, surely the audience will want to know it as well.

MW: This has actually been a blessing as David's 'non-knowledge' of this subject gave David a better eye for what the audience will want, providing

Born Ho Tsung-Tao in Taiwan, Bruce Li's family was wealthy. His grandfather was the principle of an elementary school in the 'Japanese era'. The family's money was all taken away, though, and Li's father, unfortunately, wasn't very successful financially, so Li's family had a hard time.

Li went to four different elementary schools, and suffered from red/green colour blindness, which meant that he couldn't study film or medicine. He had the opportunity to study english, history, or geography, but he was not interested in those subjects, so he ended up studying physical education instead. Li enjoyed doing gymnastics and boxing with his classmates, and he eventually went to the University of Sport. After he graduated, Li applied for and got accepted on the training course at the Taiwan Film Institute. After he graduated from there he worked on some movies, after he was discovered by Taiwan's independent martial arts movie maestro, Joseph Kuo. Li joined the army and served for 2 years, before returning to make more movies.

Li is, of course, most famous for the Bruceploitation films he made. Li was the lead in the first Bruceploitation biopic, 1974's *Bruce Lee - The Dragon Story* (aka *Super Dragon*), which was released in the United States by Allied Artists, who also released Li's Bruceploitation pic, *Bruce Lee, We Miss You!* (1975). Allied Artists was hit with lawsuits by Linda Lee for using her late husband's image in the ad campaigns for both of these movies! Another one of Li's Bruce Lee biopics, *Bruce Lee: The Man, the Myth* (1976), was very, very successful in America.

Li starred in a whole bunch of Bruceploitation movies, including *Goodbye Bruce Lee: His Last Game of Death* (1975), *The Dragon Lives* (1976), *Exit the Dragon, Enter the Tiger* (1976), *Bruce and the Iron Finger* (1979), and *Fist of Fury Part III* (1979).

Li is definitely the Bruce Lee impersonator many fans like the most. He obviously used the usual Lee mannerisms in his Bruceploitation movies, but he tended to not go overboard with them, thus he usually avoided coming across as too cartoony in his portrayals of Lee.

Bruce Le may have had the rangy, just-muscle-and-bone physique that was closer to Bruce Lee's own body-type, and Dragon Lee, with his Bruce-Lee-on-steroids body, certainly made a strong first impression whenever he appeared on-screen, but Bruce Li was the clone who, somehow, had the most presence. Some actors are fortunate that the camera loves them, and I think Li is one of those lucky folks. Bruce Le, who is a far better martial artist, can go berserk on screen, performing some brilliant moves that are great to watch, but when he's not fighting he kind of fades into the scenery. Bruce Li, on the other hand, still commands attention even when he's not in the middle of an action scene. He just didn't have to try too hard, and I guess it also helped that Li was a good-looking guy!

When Li stepped away from the film industry, focusing on bringing up his family, he became an accredited osteopath with his own clinic. He still does this and he also teaches physical education to children and the elderly.

So did he mind being called 'Bruce Li'? "My Chinese name is Ho Chung Tao," says Li. "My English name is James. The stage name they have given me is Bruce Li. I don't like Bruce Li because it feels like I am cheating, but that is what they named me, I have no way to change it." Well, I don't think he should feel too bad about this: in his interviews it is obvious that he is the 'clone' actor most respectful of Lee's legacy and the one least interested in being a celebrity... and, as the action star named 'Bruce Li', he impressed hordes of kung fu fans, who still think he's totally awesome!

A smiling Bruce Li during the filming of *Enter the Clones of Bruce* (2023)

Bruce Le is Chinese-Burmese, born Huang Kin-Lung in Burma (Myanmar) in 1950. Like some of the other Bruce clone actors, Le actually knows martial arts. He started learning at around the age of 10. His elder brother and other family members were already practicing martial arts and he followed them. He learnt karate and Burmese boxing later at his school (unlike Thai boxers, Burmese boxers don't wear gloves). He also learnt White Crane Kung Fu.

With the Chinese being persecuted in Burma, Le's family moved to Macau. Le knew nothing except kung fu, so he opened a martial arts studio and taught disciples. At that time a lot of his disciples were casino bodyguards, so he taught them practical combat skills. Another one of his disciples knew director Lo Wei...

Lo Wei came to Macau to meet Le and asked him if he was interested in becoming an actor. He asked Le to pose for some photos and sent the shots back to Hong Kong. Soon after Le was asked to go to Hong Kong and, shortly after Le arrived there, he was contacted by Golden Harvest, who Lo Wei worked for. Then Sir Run Run Shaw invited Le for a chat, and Le was asked to go to the Taiwan Province to star in a film directed by Chang Che, but Le had to refuse, the reason being that he did not have a Hong Kong ID card at that time. Le joined Shaw Brothers, signed a contract, and made films such as *Rivals of Kung Fu*, directed by Wong Fung. Le admits that at the time he

found film shooting boring because there were no fighting scenes. After 10 days of shooting *Rivals of Kung Fu*, which had martial arts choreography by Leung Siu-Chung, Le was assigned to a fighting scene with two Taiwanese actors with excellent combat skills. As Le didn't have previous experience doing film fighting, he ended up accidentally breaking one of the actor's legs - and the other actor hurt his hand when he punched Le's abs! In a later scene Le was required to fight with Shih Kien who was afraid that Le would hurt him, so he taught Le how to do a combat scene for the movies. During this period Le's name was Wong Kin-Lung.

Le began to feel that there were too many people to compete with in Shaw Brothers, and he couldn't do the types of things he liked, so he decided he wanted to leave. He eventually signed another contract and Shaw Brothers were okay with that. He went to the Philippines to shoot *Return of Bruce* and the producer asked him to use the name Bruce Le, which he did.

Le made a lot of Bruceploitation films, including *Bruce's Deadly Fingers* (1976), *The Big Boss Part II* (1976), *Bruce the Super Hero* (1979), *Challenge of the Tiger* (1980) and *The Clones of Bruce Lee* (1980). Le has been asked if he thought he was similar to Bruce Lee, and Le replied that he imitated Bruce Lee's martial art moves, but he also tried to show Bruce Lee's spirit in his movies too. "Imitating his

Bruce is interviewed in *Enter the Clones of Bruce*

soon: "There are still many people who miss Bruce Lee," Le says. "People imitate him, but no one could really be him. That's because he has become a classic. You can't even do what he did when you watch his films today, because he's got great moves and great spirit. In fact," continues Le, "he was not just a martial artist. He was an actor. He had a lot of things, his philosophy. Every move he made was like dancing, so graceful that you couldn't do it even if you tried really hard. That's because, over the years, he had made it a part of his blood and his bones."

appearance is meaningless," said Le, pointing out that what was crucial also was the need to try and show Bruce's spirit as well.

Le has, of course, been a martial arts choreographer too, sometimes because of necessity. The budgets on his movies were low and, if he was in charge of arranging the hiring of the choreographers, Le would often find that he could not afford to hire people, so he choreographed the fights for his opponents and himself. The fights were usually designed during shooting rather than beforehand.

Compared to, say, Bruce Li, it can be argued that Le didn't quite have the movie star looks. "I didn't apply much makeup for shooting," Le has admitted, "because I believed that audiences focused on my facial expressions and the power of my kung fu instead of whether I looked handsome." Le has even said that when he made *Challenge of the Tiger* it was a conscious decision to have a 'sergeant and an assistant' scenario, similar to Britt Reid and Kato in *The Green Hornet*, with Richard Harrison playing the handsome guy who attracted the women. So it seems Le was a realist when it came to evaluating his own looks.

There are still loyal Bruce Le fans after all these years, and Le has been asked why he thought this was so? "People watch it as long as it's good," said Le. "Just like singing, your voice is different from others, and it's very pleasant to listen to. It's the same for action." Is it because he looked like Bruce Lee? "No, many people do, and many people make films," said Le, who suggested that people chose to watch him because he had confidence and knew that viewers of his films would always come back to watch more. He explained that this was because he had confidence in himself, which helped him to then be successful on-screen.

With the resurgence of interest in Bruceploitation films, and with the imminent release of a box set by Severin Films, Le's audience is poised to expand even more, reaffirming his lasting impact on martial arts cinema. But does Le think that the Bruce Lee craze will, one day, be officially over? Le points out that the kung fu/Bruce Lee craze will not be over any time

WHEN RICK BAKER MET BRUCE LE...

I had the privilege of meeting Bruce Le in 2023 when I received an invitation to attend a dinner in celebration of the completion of the documentary *Enter the Clones of Bruce* by Severin Films. It was the concluding segment of filming, and Bruce was in excellent spirits.

Bruce appeared to be in fantastic shape, exuding a lot of warmth and approachability. Meeting one of the iconic Bruce Lee clones, whose films had been a staple of my viewing experience since the days of visiting the local video shop, was a truly memorable experience for me.

DRAGON LEE

aka
Keo Ryong
Moon Kyoung-seok
Bruce Rhee

CLONE PROFILE

Rick Baker fills you in on all you need to know about Dragon Lee

Dragon Lee, born Moon Kyoung-seok in Korea, is a martial arts star renowned for his prolific contributions to the Bruceploitation sub-genre. Often credited as Keo Ryong, he trained in taekwondo with Kim Tai-Chung, known for his role as Bruce Lee's double in posthumously filmed scenes for *Game of Death*. Moon also trained in hapkido with Hwang In-Shik, who is familiar to martial arts movie fans as the Japanese fighter defeated by Bruce Lee during the finale of *Way of the Dragon*. But it is interesting to note that, despite these connections, Moon actually got into the movie business when the man who painted the billboards at his local cinema told him that he resembled Bruce Lee and introduced him to a Korean film studio.

With a muscular physique and impressive fighting prowess, he looked good on screen as the rechristened Dragon Lee, standing out from many of the Bruce Lee impersonators and captivating audiences with his electrifying performances.

In 1977, *The Real Bruce Lee*, a South Korean movie, provided a platform for Dragon Lee to showcase his talents alongside a tribute to Bruce Lee himself. This film begins with a bio of Bruce Lee, then features re-dubbed clips from some of Bruce Lee's old childhood films, then it shifts to the feature-length martial arts film *Last Fist of Fury*, starring Dragon Lee, which was a notable knockoff of Bruce Lee's iconic movie *Fist of Fury* (1972).

Dragon Lee's filmography expanded rapidly as he became a staple in Bruceploitation movies, starring in titles like *Enter Three Dragons* (1978), *The Clones of Bruce Lee* (1981) and others, some of them made by Hong Kong producers Tomas Tang and Joseph Lai. Despite being labeled as a Bruce Lee imitator, Dragon Lee carved out a niche for himself, delivering captivating fight sequences and leaving an indelible mark on the martial arts film genre.

Other names he has been billed under include Bruce Lei in 1978's *Bruce Lee's Ways of Kung Fu*, and he was even labelled Bruce Rhee (!) on all the American ads and posters for the very enjoyable Bruceploitation flick *Kung Fu Fever* (1979).

Today he remains an iconic figure in martial arts cinema, helped by a resurgence of interest in the Bruceploitation sub-genre that has been reignited by websites like The Bruceploitation Blog, and now with the Severin Films doc *Enter the Clones of Bruce*, where he is one of the main interviewees. In this feature-length documentary he admits that he was not particularly proud of being a Bruce Lee impersonator, but he does acknowledge that he was the lead in a lot of movies because of this, and he muses that, maybe, he helped some people get over the loss of Bruce Lee.

The fact is Dragon Lee always looked great on-screen, with an almost feline vibe to his Bruce-esque looks, backed up by a buff, pumped physique that consistently helped him to stand out from the crowd, so his legacy will certainly remain intact and he will continue to captivate audiences eager to rewatch his fight-filled films.

Dragon appears in *Enter the Clones of Bruce*

Dragon shows off his guns!

In 1948 Leung Siu-Lung, aka Bruce Leung, aka Bruce Liang, was born in Hong Kong. He started learning martial arts from around about the age of 7 or 8. Because there were too many kids in his family, his parents sent him to his grandmother, so he grew up in a single-parent household, in a place with many families living in the one building. Liang and his grandmother were frightened by some of the other tenants, so Liang promised to protect his grandmother.

There was a place that Liang passed every day after school, which taught martial arts, and every day young Liang would stand there for 10 minutes, just watching them, then he'd go home and practice. While practicing, Liang found a corner piled high with coal, so he would practice in that corner, hitting the coal all day long! When his granny found out that Liang had pulverised all her coal she beat him! So, before Liang could learn martial arts to be able to protect his grandmother, she was beating him all the time! This did mean, however, that Liang acquired a bullet-proof body from all the beatings, helping him to become a tough dude. He began practicing Wing Chun at about 15 or 16 years of age, and before that he'd learned 'Northern Style' and more. Over time Liang got very proficient in kung fu and the proof he was good at it came when some older kids, who were 18-19 years old, began kicking him very hard, especially one guy, which made Liang get mad. "I used all my power to do this one move called 'heart piercing kick' on the guy," remembers Liang. "It was so hard I made him puke, and they never beat me since."

When he was about 15 he started working at restaurants and hotels. He didn't enjoy this much, but luckily Liang had an uncle who was a kung fu choreographer, and he started taking Liang to film sets with him. Liang would make tea, run errands, that kind of thing, and by the time he was about 18 or 19 years old, he'd become a kung fu choreographer. Liang was the youngest in that position, at around the time that Bruce Lee returned to Hong Kong. During this period Liang practiced a lot: practicing at dawn, in the mountains, then, around 9am, he would come down to the kung fu studios to practice more. Then at noon he would go practice some more. All day long was like that. But after 11pm at night there were no places open to practice. "So I would find thugs on the street to pick fights with," admits Liang, "to hone my skills that way. I fought a lot of street thugs back then." He was a tough mofo!

As a choreographer Liang would improvise on the spot, sometimes because the environment was not what the filmmakers had expected, or there'd be some other issue, so Liang had to think on his feet and keep focused on what looked good for the camera.

Now, the reason there's a profile for Bruce Liang in this Bruceploitation issue is because, though he never really resembled Bruce Lee, Liang did star in one of the craziest, silliest, most enjoyable Bruceploitation films ever made, *The Dragon Lives Again* (1977): the fighting in this movie is so good!

Liang appeared in the Bruceploitation flick *Bruce and the Iron Finger* (1979), where he steals all the scenes he's in, and he was in *Fighting Dragon Vs. The Deadly Tiger* (1974), which wasn't really a Bruceploitation movie, but the US distributors made sure to mention Bruce Lee ('Move over Bruce...') on the posters! Liang's movies *Showdown at the Equator* (1978) and *The Fists, the Kicks and the Evil* (1979) were released in the USA with new Bruceploitation titles: *Lee Lives Within* and *Lee Kicks Back*. Liang, who was making movies with Angela Mao, Jackie Chan, Jim Kelly and others, was very prolific... and then, in the late 1980s, he simply vanished from the film business (because, Liang claims, he was unfairly blacklisted by Taiwan due to the fact he'd gone on an unsanctioned PR visit to mainland China).

Liang then returned to the silver screen in 2004, appearing as The Beast in the utterly amazing *Kung Fu Hustle*. Since then he's thankfully made a load more films and TV shows, and he's one of the main interviewees in the documentary *Enter the Clones of Bruce* (2023).

Bruce Liang, with a glass of wine, in *Enter the Clones of Bruce*

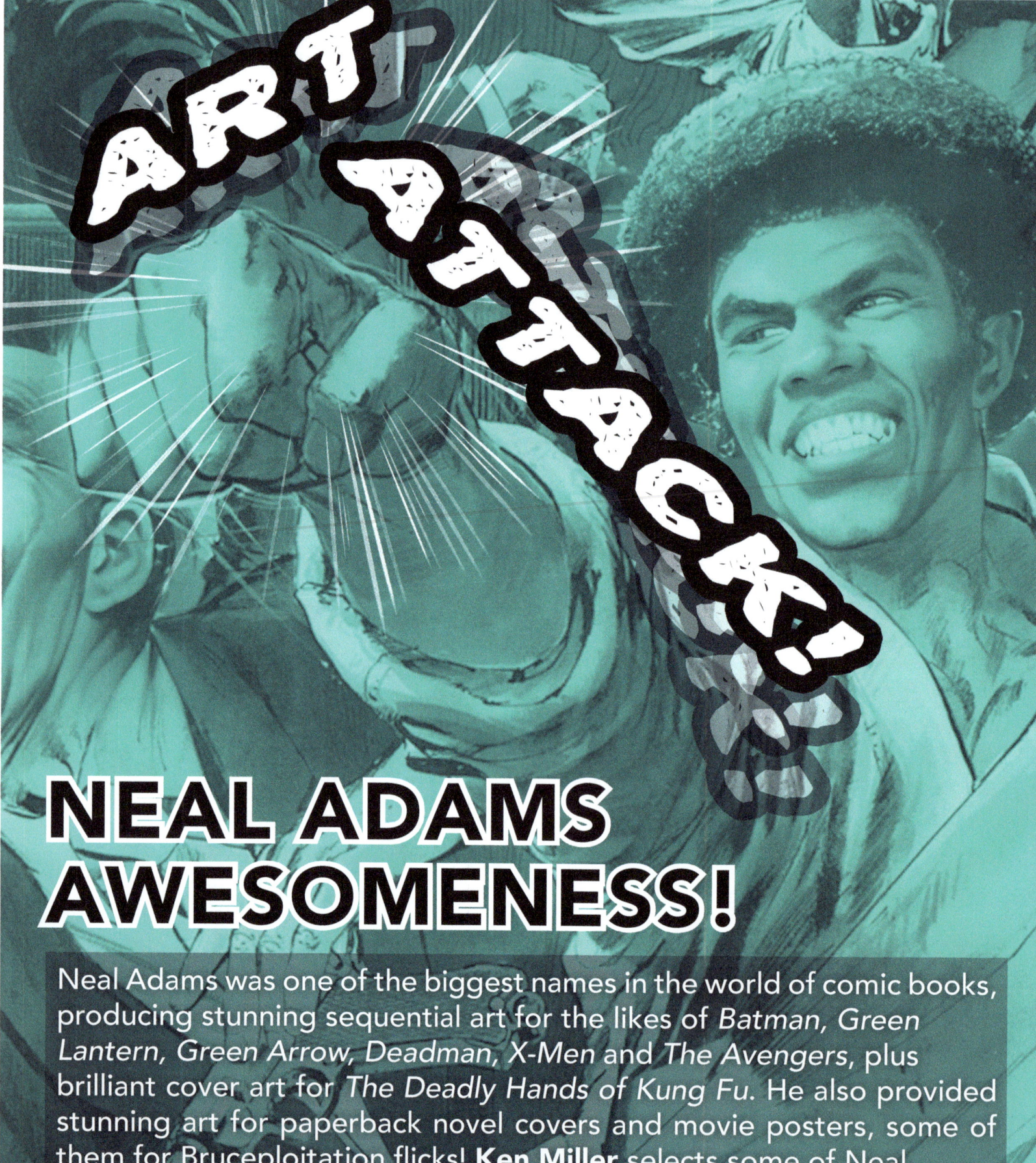

ART ATTACK!

NEAL ADAMS AWESOMENESS!

Neal Adams was one of the biggest names in the world of comic books, producing stunning sequential art for the likes of *Batman*, *Green Lantern*, *Green Arrow*, *Deadman*, *X-Men* and *The Avengers*, plus brilliant cover art for *The Deadly Hands of Kung Fu*. He also provided stunning art for paperback novel covers and movie posters, some of them for Bruceploitation flicks! **Ken Miller** selects some of Neal Adams' most kung-tastic illustration work for you to drool over...

Neal Adams was born on June 15th, 1941, in New York City. He was a student at the school of Industrial Art in Manhattan, and went on to draw humour gags for Archie Comics, worked in commercial advertising and also illustrated a daily Ben Casey newspaper comic strip. Adams finally got to draw for DC and Marvel Comics, working on such titles as *Batman*, *Green Lantern* and *The Avengers*. I first saw his work (I was a 'Marvel-only Kid' at the time) when I got my hands on issue 62 of *X-Men*. The way Adams drew the X-Men in this issue, merging dynamic, realistic anatomy with exciting, kinetic action panels, made this fantasy adventure story of superheroes venturing into a lost world of dinosaurs (The Savage Land) visually believable in a way that other artists could never have achieved. His lithe, muscled, and well-proportioned figure drawings were a joy to behold!

Splash page from issue 62 of *X-Men*. Dynamic stuff!

During his run on *Batman*, Adams and writer Dennis O'Neil really added a darker edge to the hero, which was a far cry from the lighter tales that *Batman* had been lumbered with in the wake of the very popular-but-camp Adam West TV series.

Adams and O'Neil also delved into stories that dealt with serious issues like racism, pollution and

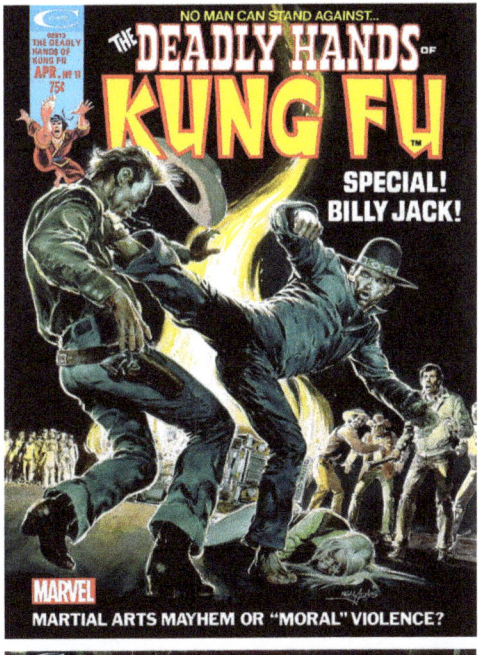

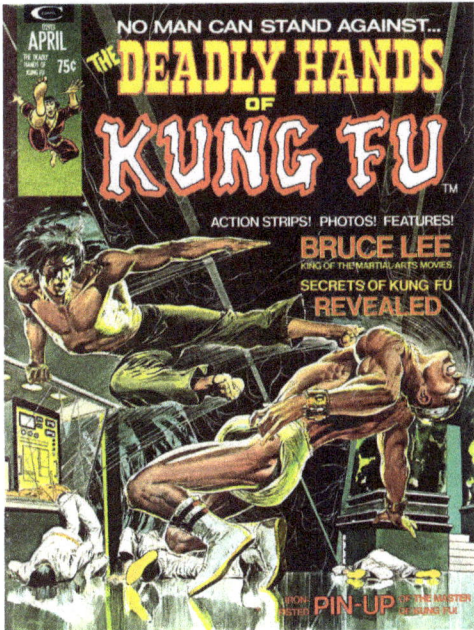

Neal Adams' wonderful rendition of the mirror maze fight between Lee and Han from *Enter the Dragon* was the cover illustration for issue 17 of *The Deadly Hands of Kung Fu*. What a stunner!

drug addiction, and they developed one of DC's first black heroes: Green Lantern superhero John Stewart.

Along with Dick Giordano, Neal Adams launched Continuity Studios, which was an artists studio that produced comic book art, movie storyboards, commercial illustration, animatics, conceptual design and posters.

Adams was a strong advocate for the rights of creators too, and worked tirelessly to promote better working conditions. He was instrumental in helping to change the practice of comic book publishers keeping an artist's original art, which resulted in policies being established that ensured art was returned to the artists, allowing the creators to sell their work and benefit from a second income stream.

Adams worked with writer Gerry Conway and penciller Howard Chaykin to introduce Killraven, a Marvel character I've always liked, in issue 18 of *Amazing Adventures*.

But let's get back to the cool, dynamic, pugilistic art that Adams produced during

the kung fu-crazed 70s...

His cover illustrations for various issues of Marvel's *The Deadly Hands of Kung Fu* were outstanding. He drew David Carradine as Kwai Chang Caine on the cover of issue 4, recreated the mirror maze fight from *Enter the Dragon* for issue 17, showed Jim Kelly beating up a Luger-toting villain for issue 3, and depicted Billy Jack in action on

This is the stonkingly splendid Bruce Lee montage illustration Adams did for issue 14 of *The Deadly Hands of Kung Fu*. Incredible work!

A great illo by Neal Adams for *Slaughter in San Francisco* - it's just a shame that Chuck Norris is hardly in the movie!

the cover of issue 11. His most impressive cover art for *The Deadly Hands of Kung Fu*, for me, was for issue 14, where he treated us to a montage of illustrations, done in varying styles in marker & paint, of Bruce Lee. Simply gorgeous-looking work!

Adams produced some of the most eye-catching martial arts movie posters of the period, including several pieces of art

Lu Chun-Ku's *The Black Dragon's Revenge* (1975), starring Ron Van Clief, Charles Bonet and Yuen Qiu, begins with lots and lots of shots of Bruce Lee newspaper clippings, so we know this is definitely going to be a Bruceploitation movie (the film's alternative titles are also dead giveaways: *The Black Dragon Revenges the Death of Bruce Lee* and *The Death of Bruce Lee*).

Neal Adams' cool artwork for the poster is a lively comic book-esque montage composition that shows off Ron Van Clief's cool afro and sideburns! There's some fight action, and a Chinese junk is included in the design to confirm that the story will involve Van Clief flying over to Hong Kong to investigate the circumstances surrounding Bruce Lee's demise.

A b&w photograph of the real Bruce Lee's dead face is used on the poster and I think this is in pretty bad taste! I'm sure that Adams had no say on what would be added to the poster. The use of actual images of Bruce Lee lying dead in his coffin was quite commonplace during the Bruceploitation era. Even Golden Harvest's more 'legit' movie *Game of Death* featured real footage from Bruce's funeral in Hong Kong.

for Bruceploitation flicks!

These film posters all benefitted from Adams' comic book-style figure drawings, giving the compositions an action-packed, pulpy vibe. He supplied US poster art for Hong Kong movies, American-produced exploitation B movies and blaxploitation actioners, and for other film genres too, including horror movies. I love his poster for 1976's creature feature *Grizzly*, which is much moodier and more atmospheric than the film it was promoting (as is often the

Killers on Wheels (1976), a Shaw Brothers Chinese biker exploitation movie, got the Neal Adams poster treatment for its US release. The design is certainly filled with incident, though it seems Adams was briefed to illustrate the characters to look like they were played by western actors.

Enter Three Dragons (1978), aka *Dragon on Fire*, starring Dragon Lee, Chang Yi-Tao and Kwok Si-Chi, was a Bruceploitation flick directed by Joseph Kong (aka Joseph Velasco), who also made the mind-bending movie *The Clones of Bruce Lee* (1980)! To add to the warped pedigree of *Enter Three Dragons*, its assistant director was none other than Godfrey Ho, the undisputed king of the cut-and-paste ninja movie genre! Class!

Neal Adams' poster art (which in no way represents what happens in the film) is comprised of four figures in a triangular composition, with the muscled, glowering Dragon Lee positioned at the front. It is very reminiscent of the classic *Enter the Dragon* poster!

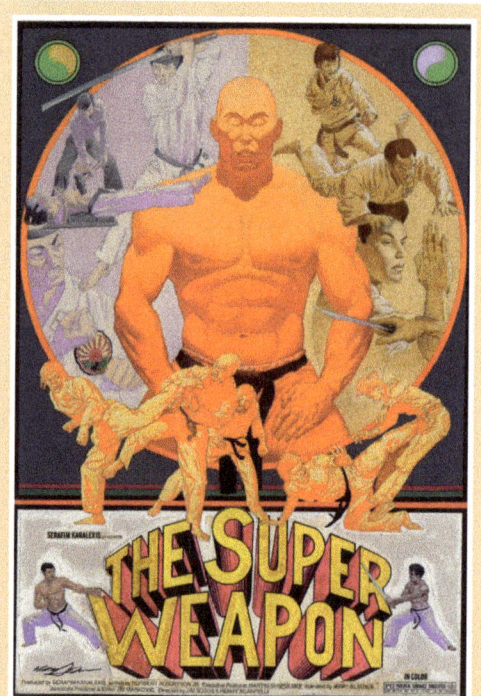

Adams gives us an interesting layout for this poster, with a zen-like, bald-headed warrior placed at its centre. This is the original artwork for *The Super Weapon*.

case, I guess).

Neal Adams won many awards and was inducted into the Will Eisner Comic Book Hall of Fame, the Harvey Awards Comic Book Hall of Fame, and the Inkwell Awards' Joe Sinnott Hall of Fame.

He was a mentor to many of the comic book industry's top creators too, including such talents as Frank Miller and also Mike Ploog.

Neal passed away in New York on April 28th, 2022, at the age of 80, after suffering

A Shang-Chi portrait commission sketch.

One of Adams' dynamic *Tarzan* paperback book covers for Ballantine.

A pen and ink Bruce Lee commission.

Let's all just agree that this poster for Joseph Kuo's *The Mystery of Chess Boxing* (1979) is ace!

complications from sepsis. With such a massive legacy of truly inspirational work, especially within the comics field, there is no chance that this very talented artist will ever be forgotten.

Neal Adams, with Dick Giordano, came up with the kind of in-your-face, colourful poster for the R-rated *Sister Street Fighter* (1974) that the grindhouse crowds of the day would really lap up: lots of punching and kicking! I'm sure New Line Cinema was very pleased with this artwork.

From China with Death (1974), aka *Wits to Wits* and *Con Man and the Kung Fu Kid*, was a kung fu buddy comedy directed by Wu Ma, starring Yu Yang, Wu Ma, Shih Kien, Yuen Shun-Yi and Chiang Nan.

Obviously briefed to play up the tough action aspects of the story, Adams supplies another one of his full-on, kinetic, montage-style compositions for this poster.

There's a lot of things happening in this artwork, including a door key being copied, the usual fluid, energetic martial arts scraps, and there's even a train. I love the nunchaku whizzing right at us!

Adams concocted an exciting cover illustration for issue 2 of *The Deadly Hands of Kung Fu*, depicting Marvel's martial arts master Shang-Chi battling a bunch of bad dudes in Times Square!

This poster for *Bruce Lee: The Man, the Myth* utilises Neal Adams illustration work and combines it with lots of photographic imagery too. I saw this movie at the cinema and it certainly wasn't "all true", but it was fun!

Finally, here's the artwork Neal Adams created for use on the US poster for *Snake in the Eagle's Shadow* (1978), aka *Eagle's Shadow*. Jackie is spelled Jacky here. This illustration is a real doozy!

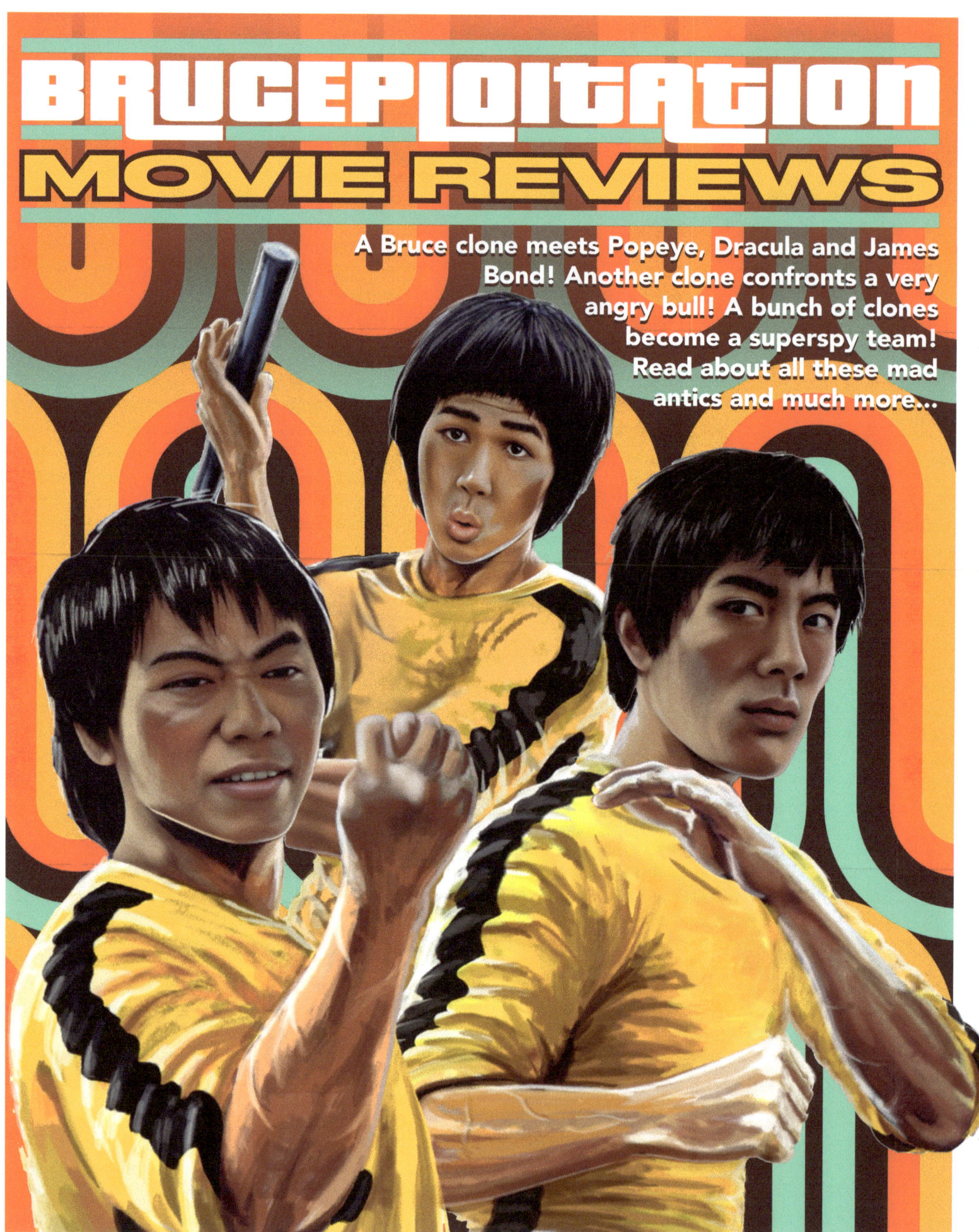

ENTER THE GAME OF DEATH (1978)

Starring Bruce Le, Bolo Yeung, Chiu Chi-Ling, Nam Seok-Hoon, Samuel Walls, John Nowell, Michael B. Christy
Written by Heo Jin
Directed by Joseph Kong
Produced by Robert Jeffery, Kim Tai-Soo
P.T. Insantra Film

Set just before World War 2, the plot involves various groups asking Chang (Le) to work for them so that they can acquire an important stolen document belonging to the Chinese government, which, in the wrong hands, could help the Japanese take over China. Le eventually joins forces with the Blue Robe Organisation and battles his way up a fighter-filled pagoda to reach a safe.

Also known as *The King of Kung Fu*, the film begins with Lalo Schifrin's *Enter the Dragon* theme tune, which then quickly becomes music from *The Spy Who Loved Me*, as we watch Bruce Le posing and posturing before a red backdrop, smashing pots and ripping open sandbags. We get freeze frames and twirling nunchucks too: what a start!

Before the later pagoda scenes, we are treated to lots of other skirmishes, as Chang takes on katana-wielding adversaries in the woods, including Bolo Yeung, who is also armed with a samurai sword. Woot! There's a fight with a group of westerners and a whole sequence set in a ring, where a crowd watches Bolo battle and beat various opponents... until Chang gets in the ring, just as another burst of the *Enter the Dragon* theme takes over the soundtrack! After some ground-grappling Chang chokes Bolo into submission, but we know they'll have a deadly rematch later in the story. ➡

Bruce Le likes to thumb his nose a lot

Thai poster that uses an image of the real Bruce Lee!

Marvellous artwork, by Kung Fu Bob O'Brien, that was used for the cover of a German Blu-ray release of the movie

Bruce Le versus Samuel Walls!

German Blu-ray cover

Bruce Le's Chang character, who likes to go for jogs wearing a *Game of Death*-style jumpsuit, refuses a lot of offers to team-up with the assorted groups that approach him, but he finally decides to choose a side after having a flashback in which he remembers when he was on the run from Japanese invaders with his cousin, who is raped by scar-faced Japanese villain Kawasaki. Extremely distraught, Chang's cousin kills herself by biting off her tongue (a somewhat common suicide method in asian films) as music from *King Kong* (1976) is played. Surprisingly, this choice of music actually works well in the scene.

The movie becomes much more off the wall once Chang enters the pagoda and encounters the exotic fighters that are awaiting him...

On the ground floor Chang comes up against a bead-throwing monk in a room full of cut-out figures used by the monk for target practice. Chang does a lot of nose-thumbing and there's a butterfly knives vs stick fight.

On the second floor Chang finds himself facing a red-haired dude in a room brimming with live snakes and (for some reason) stuffed turtles and an armadillo! Redhead throws snakes at Chang, a serpent is wrapped around his neck, and a kind of

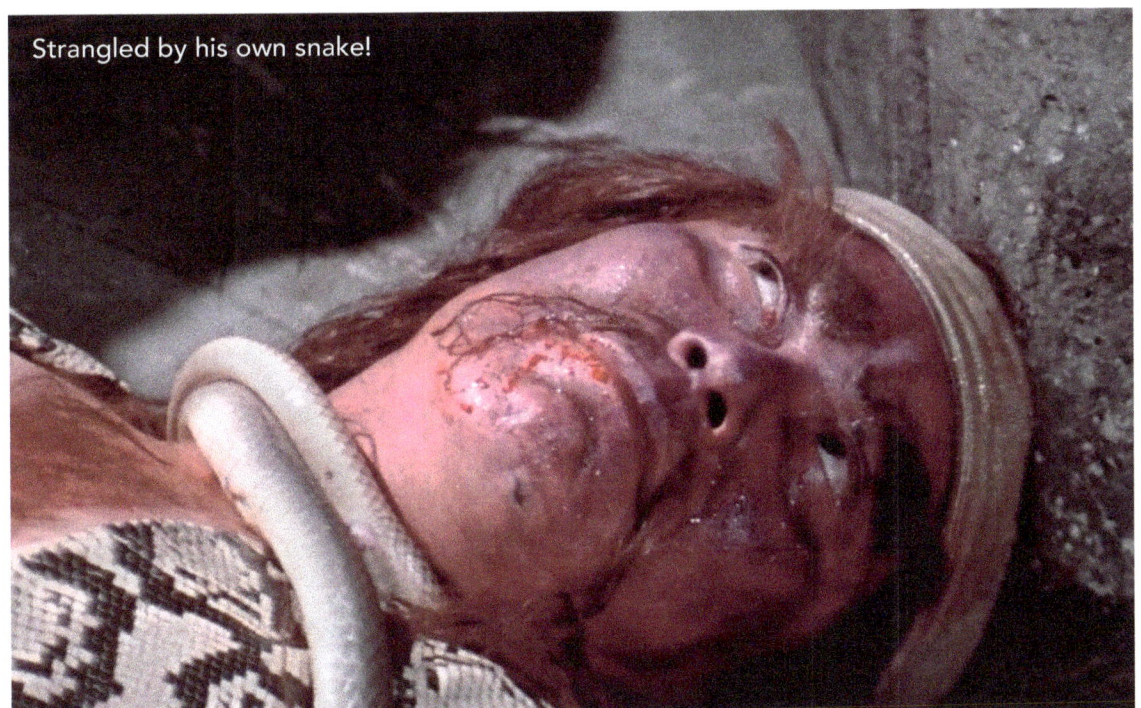

Strangled by his own snake!

were erected on an indoor badminton court, but this just adds to the enjoyment of this low budget affair. And you have got to hand it to Bruce Le for really, REALLY inhabiting his Bruce-alike role here, throwing in as many Lee mannerisms and moves as he possibly can, kitted out in anachronistic jumpsuit & trainers (this story is set in the 1930s), on his single-minded mission to be as much like Bruce Lee as possible in a film that is crammed with action.

Enter the Game of Death uses music from *Enter the Dragon* a lot, the many fights follow each other in quick succession and, honestly, there's never a dull moment!

tug of war takes place, but with a snake being used instead of a rope! After the redhead does some belly-sliding fu, he glows red when he gets injured, then bites off a snake's head and spits it on the floor... and he shoots a jet of blood from the snake's decapitated body at Chang: the blood gushes out of it like water from a garden hose! This bad guy gets his just deserts, though, when he is strangled with the corpse of his own headless snake. That'll teach him to badly treat snakes!

Chang fights a white-haired opponent next. Nunchucks are used (Chang gets his own nunchucks from seemingly nowhere) and shelves full of lit candles get trashed.

On the floor above, in a room decorated with hanging pots and white-painted posts, are two fighters, one wearing black and one dressed in white. One of the bad guys switches on a red light and informs Chang, "Red is the colour of death." Chang battles the guy in black first, then the white-clad fighter finally gets out of the bed he's been lying on, and he lashes out at Chang with extended fingers, but, of course, he proves to be no match for our hero.

Reaching the top level, Chang defeats a bearded adversary by chopping him in the throat, discovers that the document has already been taken from the safe, and exits the tower, to continue fighting thug after thug, finally beating the hell out of Bolo in a slo-mo final fight.

If you look at the floor markings in the pagoda room scenes, it becomes obvious that those sets

THE DRAGON, THE HERO (1979)

Starring John Liu, Dragon Lee, Tino Wong, Phillip Ko, Chiang Kam, Chan Lau, Bolo Yeung, Alexander Grand, Mars, David Wu, Lee Hang
Written by Sze-To On
Directed by Godfrey Ho
Produced by Joseph Lai, Tomas Tang
Martial art choreography by Tang Tak-Cheung
Asso Asia Films

The Dragon, the Hero was also known as *Dragon on Fire*, which, confusingly, is also an alternate name that was used for *Enter Three Dragons*, another Dragon Lee movie co-directed by Godfrey Ho in 1978. I hope this all doesn't confuse you!

Once again, *The Dragon, the Hero* showcases the genius of Godfrey Ho at the helm. Alongside Dragon Lee, the film features the formidable trio of John Lui, Tino Wong and Phillip Ko, making it a late night martial arts extravaganza from start to finish.

The film's opening engages viewers with a display of the key cast demonstrating their fighting styles against a red screen. It serves as a warm-up act for the audience, offering a glimpse of what to expect during the numerous fight scenes. The story unfolds 26 years after the death of their teacher, whom John Lui and Tino Wong were disciples of, learning the deadly 'Strike Rock Fist' technique. Their paths cross again when they encounter a sleazy wheelchair-bound criminal, selling priceless antiques to a Western buyer.

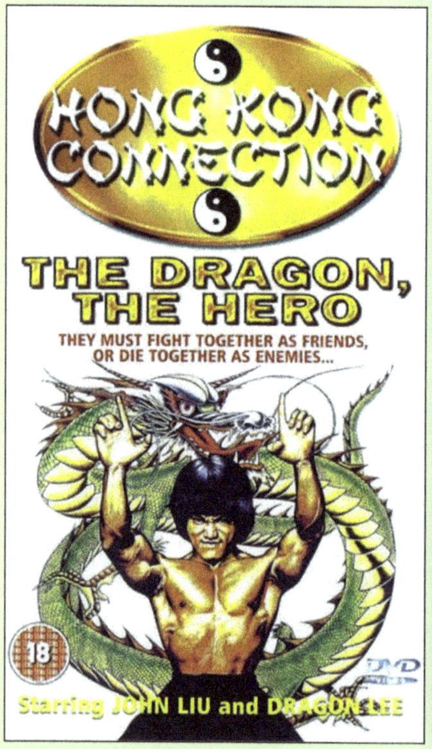

The criminal boss seeks fighters to best his champion, portrayed by Bolo Yeung as 'King Kong'. His fun introduction is marked by heavy footsteps and a camera pan revealing his hairy feet and chest wig. Should King Kong be defeated, Phillip Ko's character, the wheelchair-bound criminal's bodyguard, awaits behind a curtain. Ko's character employs a range of styles to dispatch his challengers, using an egg timer (just like the Minute Fong character does in *My Life's on the Line*) to indicate the limited time before the fight's end.

John Liu, we discover, is an undercover agent aiming to dismantle the criminal empire, infiltrating the gang by defeating its fighters. After resolving his differences with Tino Wong, Liu enlists his help along with Dragon Lee to bring down both the criminal mastermind and his bodyguard.

As one of my favourite Bruceploitation movies, released on the Eastern Heroes video label back in the 90s, watching it in widescreen was a joyous experience. The fight action is top-notch and would have surely delighted the late night cinema audiences. Despite its success in American Chinatowns, the film owes its popularity more to its cast than being a Bruce Lee movie rip off.

The film boasts outstanding fight set pieces choreographed by Tang Tak-Cheung, known for his work on Shaw Brothers films. Dragon Lee embodies Bruce Lee's essence in *Big Boss* mode, executing his mannerisms effectively. Notably, the film reveals the reason behind the gang boss' wheelchair-bound state, in a flashback where we see him force himself on to a young girl, who is rescued by her dog, which quickly removes the villain of his manhood, leaving him in a wheelchair and in a constant state of semi-rabies, acting like a dog when upset! This is a bizarre yet memorable element to the story!

Super-kicker John Liu delivers a remarkable performance, showing off his flexible 'Northern Leg' kicking and lethal 'Mysterious Hand' technique, that he boasts becomes more powerful by the hour.

This film, a dream come true for kung fu movie enthusiasts, combines 70% martial arts action and extreme training sequences with a Sam Seed look-alike who smokes 10 roll-up cigarettes (five in each hand), drinks copious amounts of wine from a gourd and also takes puffs on a opium pipe, adding to the all-round entertaining nature of the movie.

The Dragon, the Hero will appeal to fans of Bruceploitation and those fond of old-style kung fu late night action.

BRUCE AND THE IRON FINGER (1979)

Starring Bruce Li, Name Misaki, Bruce Liang, Ku Feng, Fang Yeh, Chou Chiang
Directed by Tu Lu-Po
Film Line Enterprises

A killer skilled in the Iron Finger Technique murders people with his deadly digits, which can scratch and puncture flesh, and leave two finger-holes in victims' throats that resemble vampire puncture marks.

A cop called Bruce (Li), who is an ex-kung fu teacher, becomes involved in the murder case. He goes undercover as a teacher at a kung fu school in his search for the Iron Finger killer, interviews various suspects, and gets involved in numerous punch-ups.

Even though the identity of the murderer is pretty obvious, the whodunnit/policier aspects of the story add a novel element to this kung fu flick, which is also known as *Iron Finger* and *Bruce Against Iron Hand*. Li, who plays Bruce as a stoic, righteous, kung fu-skilled dude, crosses paths with various colourful characters, including bad girl Lulu, who likes to wear transparent nighties and is involved in trafficking Vietnamese refugees with her lover Hu Pao (Feng). Hu Pao is an exponent of a kung fu style that prevents him from having sex with LuLu because doing so could kill him, so he gets angry when the libidinous LuLu keeps taking lovers and gets them to do kinky things like pretending to be a horse for her to ride and spank!

Another suspect is a martial arts teacher played by Bruce Liang, who ends up fighting Bruce Li in a rooftop scrap that's great to look at and is made even more enjoyable to watch because of a third character who keeps trying to get between them to stop the fight, but he gets punched and kicked every time he tries to do this!

Bruce Liang, with his bright red tracksuit, good-looking kicking and his novel pressure point attack technique, steals all the scenes that he's in. He becomes Bruce's ally and accompanies him to a large container port for a pugilistic showdown with the bad guys. Woot! Liang raises his fingers high like a matador and brings a fun, flamboyant jokiness to his fights with the various goons. Li, as Bruce, wearing double denim, has a more straight-faced showdown with Hu Pao, who is a real handful to fight, even when Liang joins in to help Li out.

Director Tu Lu-Po (To Lo-Po) does a good job with this film, handling scenes well, including a sequence where Bruce paces around a large scrapyard, looking for a cap-wearing villain, as Pino Donaggio's

A gorgeous Italian poster

Carrie score plays on the soundtrack. The director is aided by top-notch fight choreography courtesy of Bruce Liang and his brother Tony Leung Siu-Hung. The fast-paced martial arts skirmishes peppering this movie are all a joy to watch.

The film, with its mix of kung fu action and giallo murder-mystery trimmings, doesn't really need to depend too much on any overt Bruceploitation gimmickry, so it's no surprise that Li only does the occasional Bruce Lee battle-squeal here and seems content to do things his own way, rather than try to ape Bruce Lee too much.

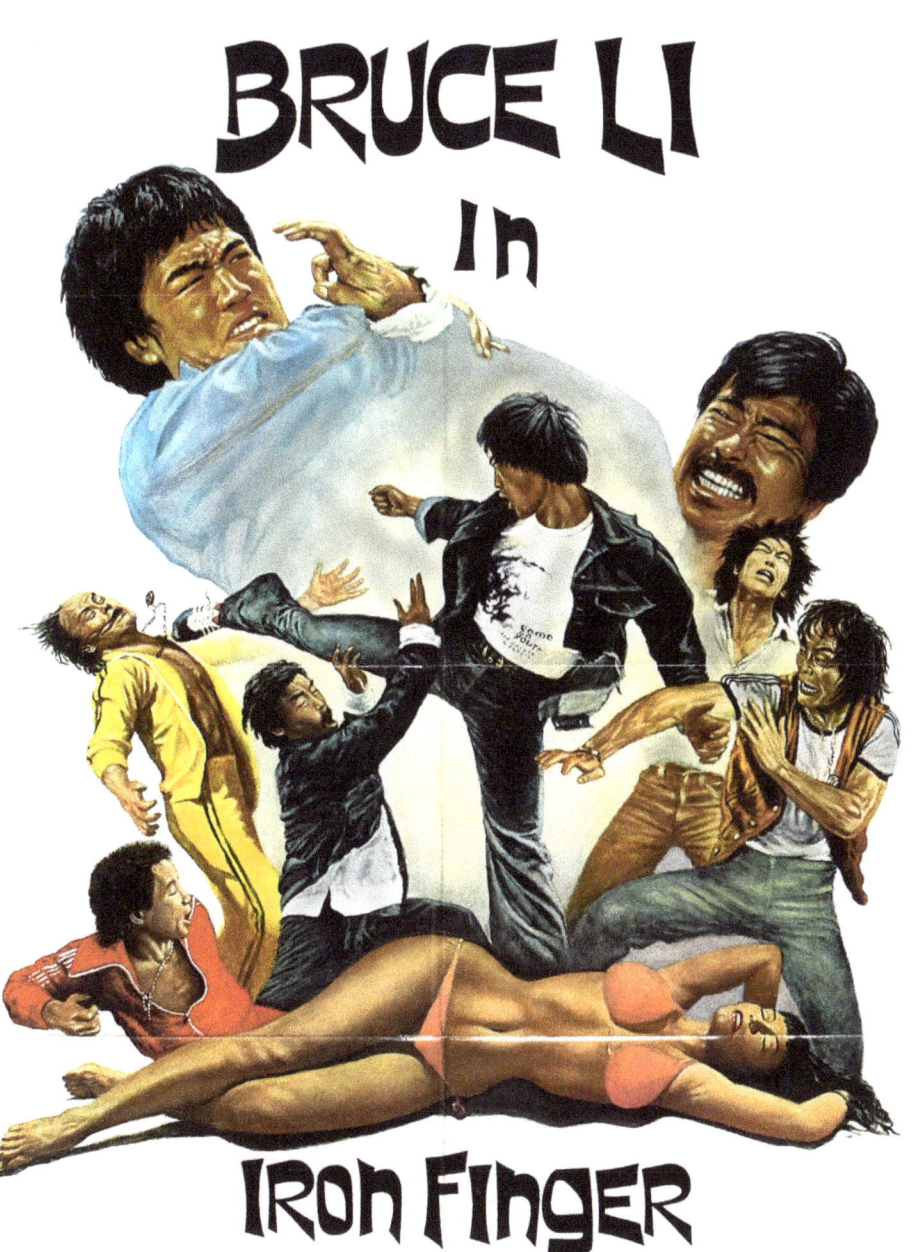

Another nicely painted poster

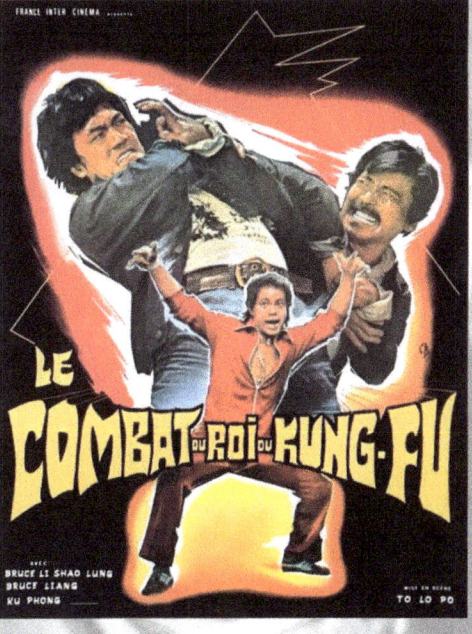

French poster

THE BLACK DRAGON VS. THE YELLOW TIGER (1974)

Starring Tong Lung, Wang Fei, Yim Chung, Jacky Chen Shao-Lung, Sung Gam-Shing, Clint Robinson
Written by Yang Yang, Chow Chen-Kon
Directed by Yang Yang
Produced by Yeh Ying-Han
Foo Hwa Cinema Company/Ming Hua Film Company

This Taiwanese production opens up with stock footage of London (for no apparent reason). The narrative unfolds as a criminal syndicate seeks vengeance for the death of one of their fighters, known as No.9. Their relentless pursuit of the character Tang Lung (who we never see), the target of their retribution, knows no bounds, as they deploy various groups of fighters to eliminate him.

Enter Tong Lung, who is Tang Lung's cousin, who assumes his cousin's identity to divert the attention of the pursuing gangs. He faces and defeats numerous adversaries sent to apprehend him, and the syndicate's main boss grows increasingly frustrated upon learning that the man besting his fighters is merely a stand-in. In a desperate attempt to get at Tong, they resort to kidnapping a young boy close to him. Tragically, when Tong refuses to comply, they mercilessly kill the boy, triggering a profound rage within Tong and the tables really turn as he transitions from prey to predator.

Originally titled *Growling Tiger* for its Hong Kong release, the film underwent a renaming for the international market, becoming *The Black Dragon vs. The Yellow Tiger*. This early Bruceploitation film features Tong Lung, credited in the titles with the same name as his character. Tong, the brother of renowned martial arts actor Alexander Lo Rei, appeared in various films alongside his bro, including *Ninja in the USA* and *The Super Ninja*.

In this movie the filmmakers have Tong Lung playing a relative of Bruce Lee's character from *The Way of the Dragon*, who was called Tang Lung. The No.9 character who is talked about by the bad guys is meant to be Colt, played by Chuck Norris, who was famously defeated by Bruce Lee/Tang Lung in the iconic colosseum fight scene, so in *The Black Dragon vs. The Yellow Tiger* the murder of No.9 is what sets in motion the syndicate's need for vengeance. Due to legal constraints, of course, this film could not be officially labelled as a sequel.

Putting all that aside, this movie does provide us with some solid one-against-many fights, something that was often seen in films of this era, where the protagonist frequently engaged gangs rather than

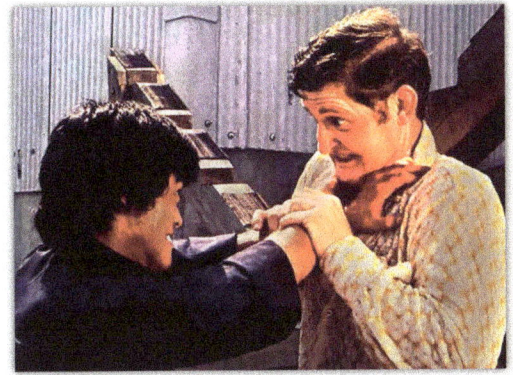

individual opponents. The fight scenes, reminiscent of the skirmishes located in spacious green gardens in Bruce Lee's *The Big Boss*, boast some commendable moments, thanks largely to Tong Lung's impressive fighting skills and Jacky Chen's adept action choreography. Tong Lung's muscular physique exudes power in every confrontation, although his handling of nunchakus could use some refinement, even though they sporadically use Lalo Schifrin's *Enter the Dragon* theme to enhance his lack of ability.

Yang Yang, who also co-wrote the script, only directed this one film, as he focused mainly on acting in films like *Mysterious Snake Women* (1974). Judging by the evident editing flaws, it seems wise that Yang concentrated on his acting. However, despite its shortcomings, the film manages to salvage some enjoyment through the aforementioned exhilarating fight scenes.

Amidst the numerous confrontations with a colourful array of assailants, including two white-suited gangsters reminiscent of Al Capone, a rotund Thai fighter, a skilled fencer, and a taekwondo expert sporting a Hitler moustache, the true essence of the film emerges in the climactic showdown...

Here Clint Robinson, portraying the Black Dragon, brings authenticity to the role thanks to the fact he's actually a real-life Grandmaster in taekwondo. His imposing presence at the top of a concrete pagoda, suggestive of Bruce Lee's *Game of Death*, adds an intriguing dimension as he claims to be Chuck's brother. The ambiguity of the term 'brother' does leave room for interpretation, and we must remember that detail was clearly not a priority in such films!

The movie is more entertaining than you might anticipate, as the dubbing, particularly by Clint Robinson, adds a layer of unintentional humour, while the acting is predictably wooden-but-fun. The plot's flaws are undeniable, failing to capture the essence of the best Bruceploitation productions but, nevertheless, the film exudes a certain charm, offering a nostalgic glimpse into the kung fu movie scene of the 1970s with its funky music, its sparse plot and its abundant fighting sequences. What's not to enjoy?

RAGE OF THE DRAGON (1980)

Starring Dragon Lee, Carter Wong, Choe Min-Gyu, Il Choi, Jang Jeong-Kuk, Jeong Ju-Hyeon, Kim Ji-Hye, Lee Seok-Goo
Written by Lee Jung-Keun
Directed by Kim Shi-Hyeon
Produced by Joseph Lai, Thomas Tang
Fight Choreography Tang Tak-Cheung
Asso Asia Films

Also known as *Mission for the Dragon*, this film catapults viewers into a world where every knock on the door could spell trouble. As the film opens, a man storms in, hurling accusations of grave robbing at the owner, who vehemently denies any involvement. But before you can even take a breath, you are thrust into a whirlwind of martial arts mayhem, with punches and kicks flying in a dizzying array of styles.

This gem from the early 80s era of Bruceploitation cinema proves to be a standout amidst a sea of imitators. Dragon Lee takes centre stage in this film as the quintessential kung fu student driven by vengeance, a role he sinks his teeth into with ferocity. Discovering his father's brutal murder, Lee's character embarks on a journey fuelled by determination and a resolve forged in the fires of martial arts training.

Adding depth to Lee's journey is the introduction of his master, a mysterious figure clad in a black costume and mask. The unmasking of the master reveals the traditional white-haired elder, sometimes humorously referred to as the 'Silver Fox' in late-night movie circles, who, after testing Dragon's skill, informs him he is ready to go forth.

Opposing Lee is the formidable Carter Wong, renowned for his iconic role in *The 18 Bronzemen* (1976), who steps into the shoes of the chief villain with chilling conviction. And while their inevitable showdown may be predictable, it is no less electrifying, serving as a testament to the genre's enduring appeal.

One notable aspect of *Rage of the Dragon* is Dragon Lee's evolution away from mere mimicry of Bruce Lee. While his physical resemblance to the martial arts legend is often striking, Lee's fighting style became increasingly distinctive, and his own flair and prowess is showcased here. This shift adds depth to his screen presence, making his combat sequences not just impressive but also uniquely captivating.

However, what truly sets *Rage of the Dragon* apart isn't just its familiar plot beats or adrenaline-pumping fight sequences, it's the sheer energy and charisma of its leads. Lee exudes raw power, his every movement pulsating with intensity, while Wong oozes menace, creating a dynamic tension that crackles on screen.

The movie as a whole is a pulse-pounding journey through the realm of classic martial arts cinema, where honour, betrayal and bone-crunching action reign supreme. So buckle up, martial arts aficionados, because this one's an action-packed wild ride from start to finish.

Lobby card

Film Frenzy   Page 48

CAMEROON CONNECTION (1985)

Starring Alphonse Beni, Bruce Le, France L. Colletin, Ariane Kah, Emmanuel Tengna, Athanase Esso, Massa Batre, Monthe Ignace, N'Hanack Tonye
Written by Roger Fellous, Alphonse Beni
Directed by Alphonse Beni
Les Films de la Rose/Frank Films Cameroun

Cameroon Connection is a film that hops on the coattails of martial arts legend Bruce Le but is more accurately a sketchy showcase for Cameroonian actor/writer/director Alphonse Beni. While Beni might not be a household name outside certain circles, fu fans may recognise him from his role in 1987's *Ninja: Silent Assassin*, aka *Black Ninja*, a cut-and-paste action flick churned out by Godfrey Ho. Ho himself admitted that Beni essentially bought his way into the spotlight with that film, highlighting its lacklustre quality. However, *Cameroon Connection* actually plunges even deeper into the realm of cinematic mediocrity!

The movie opens with a perplexing sequence involving a woman's mysterious death, setting the stage for Inspector Beko (played by Alphonse Beni) to lead the investigation. Beko's unconventional methods involve him having nightclub brawls and questionable relationships at the same time as he attempts to solve the case. His path crosses with Bruce (portrayed, of course, by Bruce Le), whose involvement adds another layer of intrigue to the plot. As Beko navigates through a web of drug-dealing thugs and voodoo practitioners, the audience is simply left wondering about the significance of it all.

Viewing the film with English subtitles saved me from the awful dubbing typical of these low-rent movies, and some of the subtitling is hilariously out of touch with today's standards, adding an unintentional layer of amusement. That aside, it's evident that *Cameroon Connection* falls short in every aspect. The plot, if one can call it that, lacks coherence, leaving viewers bewildered and frustrated. Bruce Le's physical prowess is evident, though, and he undeniably shines as the one watchable aspect of the film, with his fighting skills on point. However, the ineptitude of his opponents and Beni's laughable fight scenes, including one where he brawls with a Jim Kelly lookalike in a bar, detracts from any semblance of credibility. Beni's portrayal of Beko as a clumsy fighter further undermines the low budget film's already shaky foundations.

Cameroon Connection is such a cinematic misfire that one can't help but question Bruce Le's involvement, but, even with his presence, the movie fails to rise above its dismal premise. If there's a bottom to the barrel, *Cameroon Connection* digs beneath it, showcasing a level of incompetence

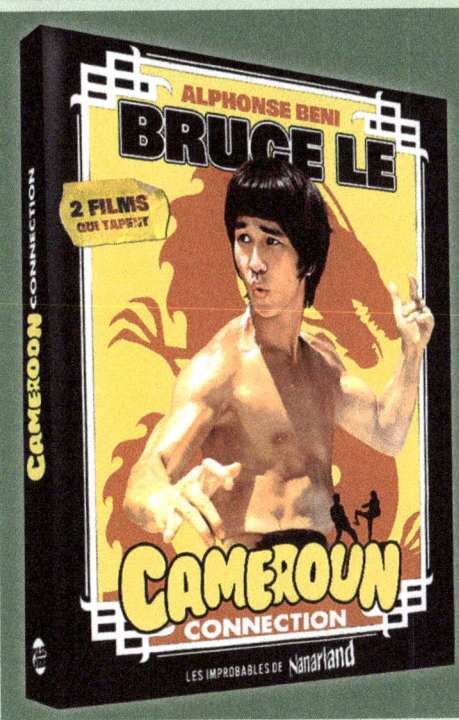

rarely seen in cinema. It's a forgettable venture into the world of action flicks that serves as a cautionary tale about the perils of vanity projects. However, for enthusiasts of the Bruceploitation sub-genre, *Cameroon Connection* is a movie that completists will want to watch and tick off, and, for folks who love to watch Bruce Le's prowess at beating up the bad guys, this flick at least has that in its favour.

KUNG FU FEVER (1979)

Starring Dragon Lee, Ron Van Clief, Choe Min-Gyu, Amy Chum, Shih Chung-Tien
Written by Ni Kuang
Directed by Kim Shi-Hyeon
Producer Yeo Ban-Yee
Yangtze Productions

Footage of the real Bruce Lee is used at the very start, with new dialogue dubbed in, and (you guessed it) shots from Bruce's funeral are included too. All of this fairly quickly gives way to the main plot, concerning the hunt for Bruce's book of finger techniques.

The protagonists and antagonists involved in this yarn include: Rickie Chan (Dragon Lee), who's the hero, Mr Ma, who is bankrolling a Moulin Rouge-type stage show, Iron Head, who fights using his bald bonce as his primary weapon, Ron (played by Ron Van Clief), who has a concealed garrotte wire in his watch, and Shu Mu, who is a top Japanese fighter. All these characters have one thing in common: they're looking for that bloody finger technique book!

In this film there are lots of 70s shades and open-necked shirts, and villainous Ron Van Clief's manly facial hair, which includes a mean moustache, is a thing of virile awesomeness. Dragon Lee, meanwhile, uses his full repertoire of Bruce Lee mannerisms. Nose-flicking is mandatory here!

When the car Ron is driving flies off the road and explodes I was gutted: I had wanted to see Ron duke it out with Dragon! Thankfully, Ron does return, with a bandaged head, having survived the car crash, and he does, indeed, have a furious fight with Dragon. Yay! For the finale Dragon arrives wearing his yellow tracksuit to kick some ass! Double-yay!

The plot may be less than stellar, but this movie never drags and is never boring, with enough fights, thuggery, and Bruce Lee mannerisms from Dragon Lee to keep you amused and entertained.

GOODBYE BRUCE LEE: HIS LAST GAME OF DEATH (1975)

Starring Bruce Li, Lung Fei, Shan Mao, Tsai Hung, Li Chiang, Ronald Brown
Written by Lin Bing
Directed by Lin Bing
Produced by Lo Chiu-Pi
Yu-Yun Film Co.

The movie commences by showing magazine and newspaper articles about Bruce Lee. There's old footage of Bruce Lee and Steve McQueen, quotes from the likes of James Coburn and an interview with Kareem Abdul-Jabbar, followed by a mini documentary with lots of photos and clips of Bruce Lee, then we're finally introduced to Bruce Li, who is playing a Chinese newcomer called Lee, who has been hired as a replacement for Bruce Lee to complete his final film. After around 12 minutes we get the proper start of the movie that purports to be Bruce Lee's last completed production, but, of course, he doesn't feature in it at all.

In this story Lee (Li) tries to help a woman whose husband has been stabbed. He volunteers to take a package to her son, who is a student, but Lee is actually being tricked and used as a courier to transport a box of cash for criminals. When Lee realises he's been duped he asks his brother to take the box to the cops, as Lee fights off a new bunch of bad guys, but the brother gets ripped off by his shifty girlfriend. Lee is threatened by the main villain (Fei), but he never seems to find the time to report this situation to the police, and he just hangs out with his girlfriend and scraps with yet more thugs. His fiancé's boss turns out to be a racketeer and events eventually lead to Lee being forced to fight his way up a tower of death, after the crooks say that they'll free his girlfriend if he manages to reach the top.

Several different edits of this film exist, and it is also known as *The New Game of Death* and *Legend of Bruce Lee*. The movie's most precious asset is definitely its theme tune: 'King of Kung Fu', sung by Kandy. This song is such an earworm! We hear it when Lee is shown training in a gym, and whenever a non-action scene threatens to become dull, the movie is saved by the return of this theme song, or by the inclusion of some other loud, purloined piece of guitar music, promising us that another action scene is on the way.

This is a Bruce Li film, but Bruce Lee is the star of the poster!

"He's the king of kung fu - king of kung fu

This is one of Bruce Li's earliest Bruceploitation flicks and his fighting lacks panache, but he has a solid presence that convinces you that he can look after himself. He occasionally fights in a more Bruce Lee-like manner, thumbing his nose and making Bruce Lee-esque screams. At around 55 minutes into the movie he walks into the bedroom of his ransacked apartment and quickly reappears dressed in a yellow & black jumpsuit, and this is when we know things are really going to kick off... especially when he runs toward the pagoda with the 'King of Kung Fu' song playing yet again! Excellent stuff! Yay! Whenever this tune is blaring out it makes me happy!

The opponents that Lee meets in the tower of death include a warrior armed with a katana, a black belt martial artist, a western wrestler in white shorts, who groans endlessly, and an adversary in an orange turban. Lee fights some of these adversaries with rather bizarre techniques. For instance, when he takes on the samurai-dude, Lee starts vanishing and reappearing behind his enemy, making the samurai very dizzy and confused! During his fight with the wrestler Lee spins him around and around, and again he wins by making his rival dizzy.

Once Lee reaches the top of the pagoda he faces-off against the gang boss, who proves to be handy with a whip. Some of this fight scene is shot at the top of an actual pagoda, though most of the time the tower is recreated as a series of room sets with views outside that are obviously painted backdrops.

The movie lacks a gripping plot and it does end rather abruptly, but there are some flamboyantly-edited moments, such as when we get multiple shots, seen from different angles, of an angry Bruce Li listening to a threatening phone call.

Ultimately, what wins you over and makes you like *Goodbye Bruce Lee* is the fact that 'King of Kung Fu' is regularly played throughout the film! This tune, by the croaky-voiced Kandy, is far catchier than it has any right to be! The song has been reused in *Death by Misadventure: The Mysterious Life of Bruce Lee* (1993) and is featured as the theme tune for *Enter the Clones of Bruce* (2023). This track is pure, funky awesomeness!

Italian poster

"king of kung fu - let him show what he can do!"

BRUCE LEE - THE DRAGON STORY (1974)

Starring Bruce Li, Chin Yung-Hsiang, Wei Yi-Ping, Anne Winton, Tang Pei, Robert Tai
Written by Lu Pin-Chung
Directed by Shih Ti
Produced by Chang Tai-Wai

Bruce Lee - The Dragon Story (aka *Super Dragon, The Dragon Story* and *Bruce Lee: A Dragon Story*) is a fascinating yet pretty flawed glimpse into Bruce Lee's life, marking the beginning of Ho Tsung-Tao becoming known as Bruce Li.

Released in 1974, a year after Bruce Lee's untimely death, this biopic is a cheap and sleazy but intriguing take on the legendary martial artist's life.

The film opens with a very loose overview of Lee's journey from delivering newspapers in a curiously Taiwanese-looking Seattle to his rise to stardom in Hong Kong. While the attention to detail might leave much to be desired (seeing Bruce as a Washington Post delivery boy in Seattle!), the narrative offers some amusing moments, such as an NBC producer casually strolling into Bruce's kung fu school with a tempting offer for a role in *The Green Hornet*.

Once in Hong Kong, the pace slows down quite considerably, but there are delightful nods to Bruce Lee's real-life acquaintances, including characters inspired by industry moguls like Raymond Chow and Run Run Shaw. The depiction of Lo Wei as an ill-tempered buffoon adds a comedic touch, while Anne Winton (*When Taekwondo Strikes*), who was sadly murdered in 1982, is good in her role as Linda Lee, emerging as the true mastermind behind the scenes.

The latter half of the production really delves into Lee's controversial affair with Betty Ting Pei, veering into soap opera territory with suicide attempts and self-destruction. While there are only a few brief fight scenes, Bruce Li fails to capture the essence of the real Bruce Lee at this early stage in Li's career. The fight action is also clumsy, made more so by the opponents he has to fight, though Li would

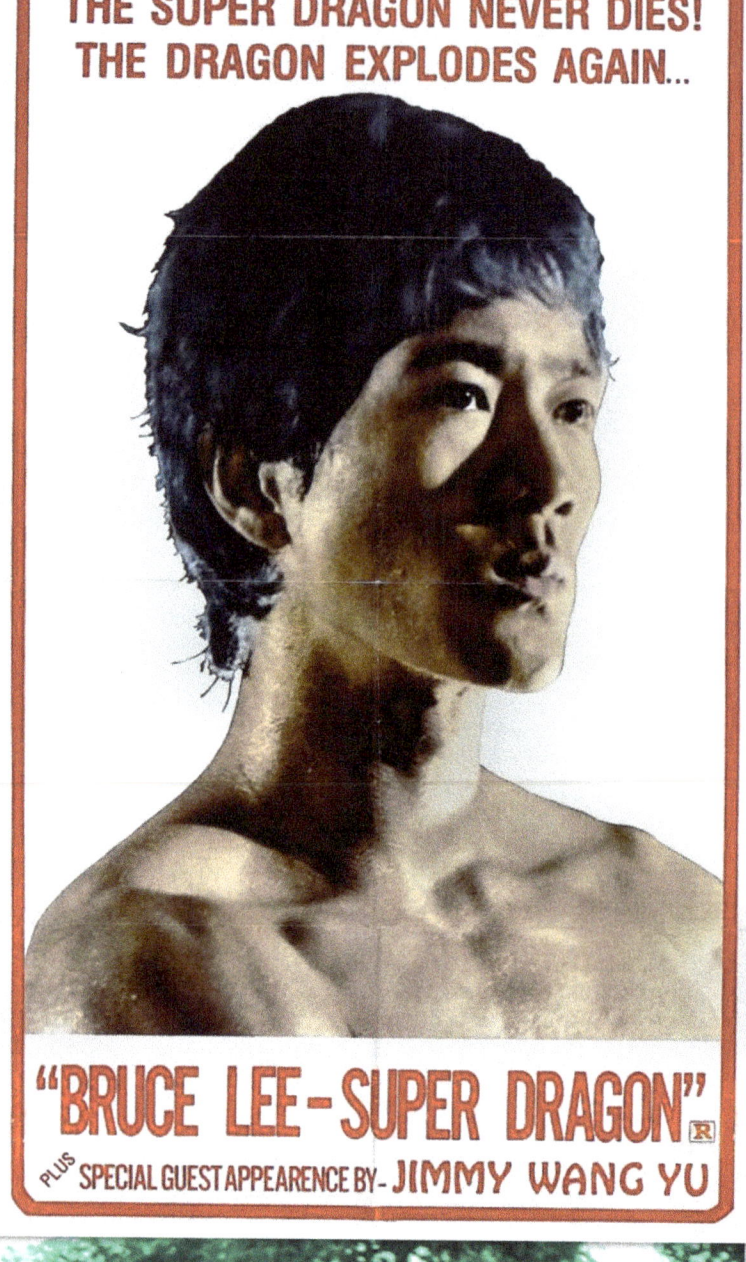

Film Frenzy   Page 52

later improve his martial arts prowess, as he developed his on-screen Bruce persona.

Interestingly, the film's focus on scandal rather than action sets it apart from later biopics like *Bruce Lee: The Man, the Myth* (1976), which opted for a more heroic portrayal of Lee as a global ambassador for Chinese kung fu. It took time for producers to realise that audiences craved the ass-kicking Bruce Lee persona over tabloid fodder.

One peculiar aspect worth mentioning is Bruce Li's sudden appearance with a moustache in one scene: that's quite an unexpected facial hair development!

Bruce Lee - The Dragon Story may not be the pinnacle of cinematic excellence, but it is a must-watch for aficionados of Bruceploitation movies seeking insight into the early days of this sub-genre.

CHALLENGE OF THE TIGER (1980)

Starring Bruce Le, Richard Harrison, Hwang Jang-Lee, Bolo Yeung, Dick Randall, Brad Harris, Sharon Shira, Nadiuska
Written by Bruce Lee, Pan Fan
Directed by Bruce Le
Produced by Bruce Le, Dick Randall
Dragon Films Company

Scientists who've developed a sterilising formula capable of killing human sperm are immediately murdered and their formula is stolen. CIA agents Richard Cannon (Harrison) and Huang Lung (Le) are sent on a mission to retrieve the deadly formula before it can be sold to the highest bidder.

This flick, directed by Bruce Le himself, is fun, fun, fun!

Beginning in Spain, the movie introduces us to Richard Harrison's character, who is called Richard, of course, as he drives his Porsche to a large residence where he plays tennis with a topless, well-endowed female player... in slow motion! Lots of other girls are there too, all topless, and soon they're fully naked, hanging around a swimming pool. Richard's carefree carnal canoodling is interrupted, however, by a phone call informing him that he's needed for the mission.

Richard and Bruce get caught up in a

Bruce likes to watch...

Bruce and the bull!

fight and a shootout, and end up at a bullring arena, where there's another exchange of fire and Bruce fights goons in the bullring itself... and then an angry bull attacks! Bruce does some Bruce Lee-style skipping in front of the black bull! After using a matador's cape, Bruce punches the bull in the head - cue a graphics illustration of a crack appearing in a bull's head - and the horned beast dies! Awesome! This is an entertaining sequence, with the bull brought to the screen via the use of a real bull and a stuffed bull.

Richard is soon hitting it off with Maria (Nadiuska), a voluptuous, sexy and shady lady who claims to be a former Miss Spain but is linked to the stolen formula caper. As Richard and Maria head for a bath, Bruce sneaks about, fights dudes, jumps over garden walls and even thumbs his nose like Bruce Lee as he watches Richard get soaped-up by Maria!

As can be seen here, in front of the camera Bruce Le plays a character with little interest in women - he's an agent who is fully focused on his job - but behind the camera director Bruce Le seems to believe that enough is never enough when it comes to showing naked female flesh!

Hwang Jang-Lee and Bolo Yeung are introduced as Vietnamese agents who also want to get their mitts on the deadly formula, which Maria now takes to Hong

Breefy bad guys say 'hi!'

Kong, where she liaises with colleagues, including Leopard (Harris), a curly-haired westerner with bulging biceps. Richard and Bruce arrive in Hong Kong too, teaming-up with redhead fellow CIA agent Anna (Shira), and the threesome decide to head to the beach. Here Richard, in his tiny, light blue budgie smugglers, beats up some guys, then makes a move on a woman who's actually a Vietnamese agent. In no time Richard has got her naked in bed with him: he doesn't mess around!

When Bolo fails an assignment, he's attacked by Hwang Jang-Lee and the ensuing fight is over pretty quickly. Bye, bye Bolo, shame you had to die so soon!

The story shifts to Macau, as the villains plan to mass-produce the formula there. Bruce and Richard are harassed by motorcyclists on stone steps, and then Bruce and others crash a fancy harness racing event, providing the filmmakers with the chance to surreptitiously shoot footage at this party, filming the likes of Jack Klugman, Jane Seymour and Morgan Fairchild. It's fun watching the actors, who

French poster

Bruce Le meets Jane Seymour!

are all in character, including a beefy, vest-wearing Brad Harris and Hwang Jang-Lee in shades, intermingling with the real-life guests of this gala event! Bruce Le even goes up to Jack Klugman to shake his hand, and does the same with Jane Seymour. Cool! This means, of course, that Klugman and Seymour are officially part of the Bruceploitation sub-genre! Various standers-by can be seen looking at the camera inquisitively and, at one point, you can check out the reflection of the film crew in Richard Harrison's shades!

Bruce Le definitely does the lion's share of the fighting in this movie, with Richard Harrison playing a kind of easy-going, semi-inept Roger Moore-style character much of the time, sending up the usually tough, macho character he plays in his other films. At one point, when Richard encounters a super-muscly dude, he just tries to run away! Once he's forced to fight this guy he is finally helped by Bruce to take the muscled menace down.

The action continues to come thick and fast, with Bruce Le and Brad Harris, both wearing black vests, having a fight that ends when Bruce blinds Leopard with his deadly poking fingers! This fun finale, set around some old fortifications, sees Hwang Jang-Lee, who doesn't do an awful lot in this movie, other than kill a few of his own team, finally taking part in a boss-level battle with Bruce Le. Hwang unleashes some of his signature kicks, then attempts to drive off with the formula in an old wreck of a car, but Le manages to send Hwang crashing to a fiery end down the side of a hill. At this point Richard rocks up, dressed in his shirt, tie and jacket, to have a final laugh with his buddy.

Okay, sure, so the plot is feather-light, existing merely to nudge the story forward, from Spain to Hong Kong, and then on to Macau, but that's just fine, because *Challenge of the Tiger* is absurd, cheesy, adventurous, semi-raunchy fun that keeps you entertained throughout.

Look out for Dick Randall, producer of Bruceploitation flicks like *The Real Bruce Lee* (1977), playing one of the bad guys.

Chinese language poster

ENTER THREE DRAGONS (1978)

Starring Dragon Lee, Chang Yi-Tao, Kwok Si-Chi, Nick Cheung Lik, Samuel Walls, Bolo Yeung, Phillip Ko, Fang Yeh, Tiger Yeung, To Siu-Ming, Alexander Grand
Written by Szeto On
Directed by Joseph Kong
Co-directed by Godfrey Ho
Produced by Tomas Tang, Joseph Lai
Asso Asia Films

Step into the realm of *Enter Three Dragons*, also known as *Dragon on Fire*, a Bruceploitation spectacle helmed by the dynamic duo of director Joseph Kong and assistant director Godfrey Ho.

Our saga ignites when Sammy (portrayed by Samuel Walls with a street-savvy charisma), a small-time hustler, gets himself entangled in a web of underworld intrigue. Seeking aid, he enlists the help of ace kung fu master Dragon Hung (Chang Yi-Tao) to navigate the chaos.

But brace yourselves, martial arts enthusiasts, for the plot now twists and turns as Dragon Yeung (Kwok Si-Chi) finds himself mistaken for the other Dragon. And if that wasn't confusing enough, another dragon arrives in the form of the very

Dig those 70's shades, man

formidable Dragon Lee, who plays Bruce Hung, Dragon Hung's kin. I hope you're following all of this!

Amidst the flurry of punches and kicks, Sammy and the various dragons (who never really meet) confront a rogues gallery of villains, including the familiar faces of Phillip Ko, Tiger Yeung and Bolo Yeung.

A special note must be given to the dubbing, which is pretty hilarious; one might think a cadre of Victorian-era cockney ruffians were part of the voice cast! And Samuel Walls' voiceover is a testament to classic kung fu movie dubbing at its zenith. Amidst the cheesy chaos, moments

Neal Adams artwork

Chang Yi-Tao, as Dragon Hung, dons a *Game of Death*-style jumpsuit for a whi

Dragon Lee, as Bruce Hung, bursts into action!

Kwok Si-Chi plays Dragon Yeung, who is mistaken for Dragon Hung

image of Bruce Lee in this flick, yet he's relegated to the sidelines without a single fight scene. A missed opportunity indeed, but at least he went on (billed as Bruce Lai) to take part in lots of action in Joseph Kong's insane movie *The Clones of Bruce Lee* (1980).

Enter Three Dragons is a fun-filled ride of martial arts madness, tailor-made for aficionados of Bruceploitation cinema and those with a keen sense of humour. And let's not forget the striking poster art by Neal Adams, channelling the iconic imagery of *Enter the Dragon* to entice international audiences.

of brilliance emerge, with decent fight choreography and infectious, borrowed tracks on the soundtrack, from the likes of Giorgio Moroder and James Bond movies, that help to elevate the scenes they're used in.

Yet, amidst the fun fight frolics, questions linger. What's the deal with Kwok Si-Chi? He's the spitting

French poster

THE DRAGON LIVES (1976)

Starring Bruce Li, Caryn White, Chen Pei-Zhen, Ernest Curtis, Joe Nerbonne, Fred Cargle, Elton Hugee, Jim Burnett, Kjell Wallen, Mark Ruth, Jack Nickelson
Written by Ni Kuang, Song Hsiang-Yu
Directed by Wang Sing-Loy
First Film Production Company/First Films Organisation/Film Ventures International

Well, slap my face with a cutout Bruce Lee mirror face! Here we have Bruce Li, the man who could mimic Bruce Lee's war cry faster than a "Whataaaaaa!", once again transforming into a Bruce clone look-alike. Not for the first time, not twice, but for quite a few times Li played Bruce in very, very loose biographical movies and action flicks. And guess what? This classic, also known as *He's a Legend, He's a Hero*, proudly stands as one of those cinematic endeavours.

Kicking off with Bruce's grand entrance as a newly born baby, coming into the world as lightning and thunder echo through the night sky, this rollercoaster opening briefly skims through his childhood before catapulting us into his young adulthood escapades in San Francisco. In one scene Bruce, asked to play an extra by a film crew, gets pissed off when they deck him out as a cliched Chinese stereotype! Bruce also wows the crowds at a martial arts showdown, taking down a towering titan spewing more anti-Chinese vitriol than a social media troll on a bad day.

But hold onto your nunchucks, folks! Hollywood beckons once more, offering our hero the role of a lifetime on a jade platter: none other than Kato from *The Green Hornet*. But, yet again, Bruce finds

The Dragon Lives was the kind of movie the grindhouse theatres really loved!

course, can happen in a Bruceploitation movie.

To be honest, the editing is atrocious, the acting is more wooden than a Taiwanese puppet show, and the story of Bruce's rise to stardom is definitely an alternative dimension's version of the true events.

The main soundtrack and the smooth theme song, 'He's a Legend, He's a Hero', is written and performed by Anders Nelsson, who incidentally wrote the music for *The Tattoo Connection* (1978), *Heroes Three* (1985) and many more film scores. And at least Anders does have an actual connection with the real Bruce Lee, as he played one of the thugs in *Way of the Dragon* (1972).

Criticisms aside, *The Dragon Lives* is all a Bruceploitation fan could want and more, with every frame tinged with the spectre of

Spanish poster

Bruce's untimely departure, from his stormy birth to dialogue more ominous than a fortune cookie prophecy: it's clear that time's ticking louder than a bomb about to go off. But fear not, for even as Bruce exits stage left, we know his legend will live on, helped in no small measure by the colourful Bruceploitation films that flooded the market after his passing.

himself recoiling and getting angry at the sight of a proposed mask and phoney Chinese ponytail he is asked to wear.

With the bitter taste of racism lingering like a stubborn ghost pepper, Bruce decides to take his talents back to the Pearl of the Orient - Hong Kong. And let me tell you, when Bruce sprouts a moustache out of nowhere, you know things are about to get wild! This results in instant success! Bruce gets it all: mansions, pools and a dog for good measure. But, hey, fame's a fickle friend, ain't it? Bruce locks himself away in a gym, sweating buckets like he's trying to outdo a sauna, much to the concern of his wife, Linda, who's probably pondering how she managed to buy such a big mansion without his knowledge. But anything, of

THE BLACK DRAGON'S REVENGE (1975)

Starring Ron Van Clief, Jason Pai Piao, Charles Bonet, Yuen Qiu, Lau Hok-Nin
Written by Norbet Albertson Jr
Directed by Lu Chin-Ku
Produced by Serafim Karalexis, Howard Mahler
Yangtze Productions

In New York the Black Dragon (Van Clief) is hired to look into the death of Bruce Lee, so he flies over to Hong Kong and, with the help of antiques shop owner (and martial artist) Charley Woodcock (Bonet), he soon finds himself fighting a variety of kung fu-skilled antagonists.

The plotting is sometimes not as tight as it should be, with superfluous dialogue about such things as a buddha ornament, and a scene with the Black Dragon pulling a rickshaw around the streets that is just a funny filler moment rather than an incident linked to the actual story. But this doesn't bother me in the slightest, because *The Black Dragon's Revenge*, aka *The Death of Bruce Lee*, is a very engaging kung fu romp.

Ron Van Clief looks cool as he struts about, wearing flared trousers and various funky, 70s-tastic tops. He's a solidly-built, cool-as-f**k mofo with an afro and manly sideburns, and he looks good on-screen as he kicks and punches his opponents. Sometimes he wears a sharp, smart suit, such as when he visits a Chinese opera backstage. Here an actress wipes the Black Dragon's face to see if his dark skin is just makeup, and Van Clief coolly replies, "No, baby, it's the real shit."

The story cuts between scenes with the Black Dragon & Charley, and other sequences focusing on another bunch of characters from a kung fu school, who have a master that likes to spout zen-style quotations. Basically, everyone is looking into the death of Bruce Lee, with shifty suspects including a fighter claiming he murdered Bruce with a killer-punch, a bogus newspaper reporter, and some vengeance-seeking drug dealers.

This is a decently-shot production peppered with fights and conversation scenes in which competing conspiracy theories concerning Bruce Lee's demise (drug addiction, drug allergies, death by assassination, etc) are raised and discussed. The stakes are raised in the story when Charley's store employee has his eyes poked out by the main villain. The methods of attack become more dangerous and exotic when a villainess starts using her poisonous snakes and blow darts. Charley, played by Charles Bonet (who gives his all as the Black Dragon's buddy), goes down fighting in an alley showdown, and the Black Dragon finally teams-up with the kung fu school mob, one of whom is Yuen (*Kung Fu Hustle*) Qiu, who has some neat kung fu scraps, twirling around a staff during one particular street confrontation.

Barechested Van Clief looks extra cool when he does a kata in the kung fu school's garden, just before he heads off to a meeting with a witness who turns up dead, thanks to a faked drug overdose. The movie soon throws in a twist reveal regarding who is ultimately the top villain behind it all, which maybe doesn't make complete sense, but this is a minor quibble as it leads to a final face-off on a beach, with tonfas and sai being brandished as the two combatants battle to the death.

The Black Dragon's Revenge is a very enjoyable Bruceploitation flick benefitting from the badass presence of Ron Van Clief: the Black Dragon!

Spanish poster

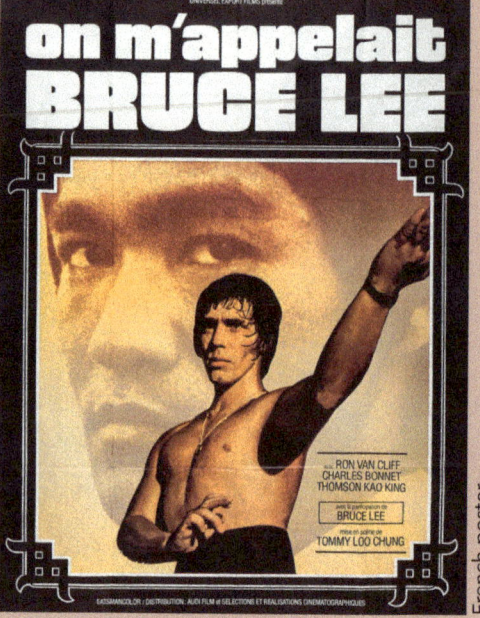

French poster

BRUCE LEE, WE MISS YOU! (1975)

Starring Bruce Li, Shan Mao, Lung Fei, Tang Chia-Chuan
Written by Yen Chung
Directed by Li Kuan-Chang
Produced by Liu Hsiao-Ling

A martial artist (Bruce Li) is totally distraught when he hears the news of Bruce Lee's passing, he drinks too much, has dreams in which he is visited by the spirit of Bruce Lee (also played by Li), and he feels compelled to look into the events surrounding the Dragon's death. After visiting a monastery, where he has to fight and beat some monks to prove to the abbot that he can look after himself, he heads off on his mission, sometimes aided by his brother, who's also a martial artist. Li eventually uncovers the truth, that a gambling ring had killed Bruce Lee because he could have somehow messed up some fight they had money on by refusing to join the top gang boss in Europe.

In this movie, also known as *Golden Sun*, Bruce Li's skills at acting drunk are not as well-honed as his skills at on-screen fighting, that's for sure! The fighting in this movie, actually, lacks finesse, but, while the action isn't of the top shelf variety, the filmmakers certainly don't scrimp on the amount of kung fu scrapping on show. There's one skirmish that takes place on a (slow moving) bus and another that begins in an urban locale, transitions to an area covered in piles of gravel, then cuts back to the urban environment.

There are scenes where Li is mistaken for Bruce Lee, which either spooks people

FIST OF FEAR, TOUCH OF DEATH (1980)

Starring Fred Williamson, Ron Van Clief, Bruce Lee (archive footage), Adolph Caesar, Aaron Banks, Mark Messina, Bill Louie
Written by Ron Harvey
Directed by Matthew Mallinson
Produced by Terry Levene
Aquarius Promotions

This is a pseudo-documentary oddity set at the 'Oriental World of Self Defense' event at Madison Square Garden, though the filmmakers would have us believe that this is actually the '1979 World Karate Championships'. Yeah, sure. Anyway, the movie soon has Aaron Banks claiming that Bruce Lee was killed with a 'touch of death', otherwise known as 'vibrating palm'. The movie tries to pass off this Madison Square Garden tournament as the place where it will be decided who Bruce Lee's successor will be.

This curate's egg really is a load of old nonsense! We have footage of Bruce Lee with new dubbed dialogue, we have reportage mixed with dramatic sequences, we have a scene where two female joggers are hassled by lowlifes... until a car pulls up and a moustached 'Kato' (Bill Louie) gets out to kick ass!

The preposterous narration includes the claim that Bruce Lee's great grandfather was one of China's greatest samurai swordsmen. WTF?! Basically, this 'fact' is used as an atom-thin excuse to use footage from a wuxia film, with the swordsman hero being passed off as Bruce's descendant. Lots of clips from this swordplay movie are mixed with LOADS of footage from a b&w Hong Kong film that Bruce Lee made when he was young. The new dub purports to have Lee's character talk about wanting to have karate lessons. "Ma, karate is our family tradition," says Bruce, and his ma has a flashback daydream about Bruce's great grandfather, thus giving the filmmakers an excuse to show yet more of that goddamn wuxia footage! This extended sequence, where the colour swordplay film clips are intermingled with the old b&w Bruce drama footage, just goes on and on! The new dubbed dialogue covers everything from speculation that Bruce's great grandfather was killed by a 'touch of death', to gossip about Bruce's girlfriend, who some family members suspect is secretly seeing the delivery boy. What?! This stupid dialogue becomes unintentionally risible, and the tenuously-linked splicing of disparate footage actually makes ANY Godfrey Ho movie look like a coherent masterwork by comparison! This entire section of the film, which includes shots of the wuxia hero fighting a midget and a dude with a large abacus, beggars belief as you reflect on the filmmakers' shameless use of mismatched stock footage to fill the running time! They also use pointless clips of Clint Eastwood, John Wayne, Raquel Welch and others on the red carpet at the Oscars!!!?

There's a sequence with Ron Van Clief, playing a boxer, hitting a punch bag as he talks about when he met Bruce Lee, then he does weights as he continues to chat about Bruce. "He was the prototype, everyone else is an imitation," says Ron.

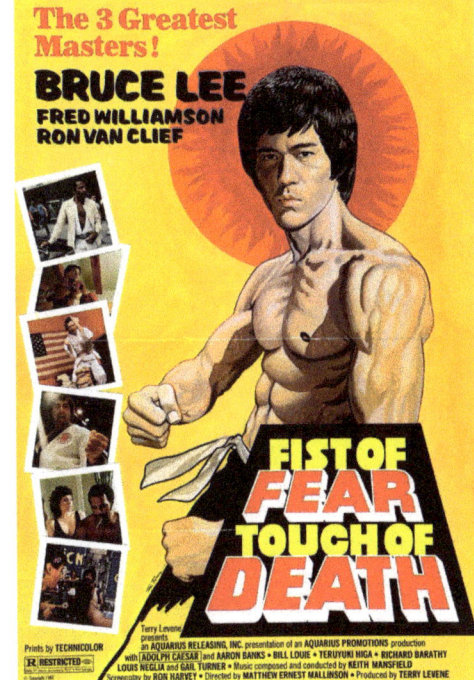

We then watch Ron beat-up four creeps leering at a female passer-by.

Probably the best portion of the film is the stuff with Fred Williamson, who has some fun at his own expense, pretending to get pissed off when folks repeatedly mistake him for Harry Belafonte!

The end fight at Madison Square Garden (supposedly to finally find out who is Bruce Lee's successor) is actually a boxing match and nothing to do with kung fu or karate, even though the film bills it as the 'World Welterweight Karate Championship'. Jeez! These filmmakers knew no shame!

or convinces them that Bruce Lee never died and that Li is actually Lee. The novel angle to this particular Bruceploitation flick, though, is the idea that Li's character is somehow possessed by the actual spirit of Bruce Lee! After having more visions of Bruce Lee, Li becomes really motivated to take on the villains. Li eventually confronts the big boss on a golf course, where the fight finale kicks off and Li somehow gets taken over by Bruce Lee! Li makes Bruce Lee noises and chases the boss away from the golf course, through a field of pampas grass and finally pursues him across the dirt slopes of a quarry... and every now and then we get to see the little image of Bruce Lee (played again by Bruce Li, of course) superimposed on Li's head! Excellent stuff!

This isn't the best Bruceploitation film out there, but it has its memorable moments, including a flashback that recreates the fateful evening Bruce Lee (played once more by Li) died on a bed at a woman friend's home: in this version of events we watch as Bruce, who has been dealt some kind of delayed death-blow, leaps around in agony. The slow motion jumping around on the bed is exaggerated to truly over the top levels and becomes silly rather than dramatic! Hey, this film's worth a watch, if only for the quick shots of lil' Bruce Lee overlaid on Bruce Li's head!

Look! The spirit of Bruce Lee is in his head!

THE CLONES OF BRUCE LEE (1980)

Starring Dragon Lee, Bruce Le, Bruce Lai (Kwok Si-Chi), Bruce Thai, Bolo Yeung, Jon T. Benn, Leung Siu-Wah, Andy Hannah, Alexander Grand, Tong Si, Cheng Kei-Ying
Directed by Joseph Kong
Produced by Dick Randall, Chang Tsung-Lung
Action by Bruce Le
Filmline Enterprises/Wai Leng Film Company

Nurses rush through a hospital with Bruce Lee's body on a gurney. A surgeon does his best to save Bruce, but to no avail. Professor Lucas (Benn) is brought into the operating theatre and he uses a syringe to withdraw blood from Bruce's dead body. The Prof soon creates three adult clones of the deceased film star: Bruce Lee 1 (Dragon Lee), Bruce Lee 2 (Bruce Le) and Bruce Lee 3 (Bruce Lai). These clones are trained, then sent abroad on assassination missions sanctioned by the Special Branch of Investigation, but, eventually, problems arise closer to home when Professor Lucas becomes power-mad...

Early on in *The Clones of Bruce Lee* there's some news footage showing clips of Bruce Lee and, as is the way with these Bruceploitation flicks, there are also some pics from Bruce's funeral, but, once that's dealt with, the movie focuses on being a diverting, sci-fi-tinged, fight-filled, silly, colourful escapade.

There isn't a long build up to the big reveal of the clones: within minutes the movie shows us Professor Lucas dealing with his Bruce clones, though how he managed to speed-grow them to instant adulthood is not explained. These clones, whilst still in the lab, aren't dressed in hospital gowns, by the way, they're kitted out to resemble Bruce Lee: they're barechested and all wear black trousers, white socks and black kung fu shoes!

Soon the clones are being trained and exercised. Bruce 1 works out to the theme from *Rocky* and one of the martial arts instructors turns out to be Bolo Yeung! Sweet! But no explanation is given for why Dragon Lee's Bruce 1 doesn't do any training with the other two Bruce Lee clones.

Bruce 1 is sent on a mission to take down movie studio mogul Chai Lo, who is using his business as a front for a gold smuggling racket. Bruce 1 must infiltrate the film studio by getting employed as a fighter in the current movie and then assassinate Chai Lo.

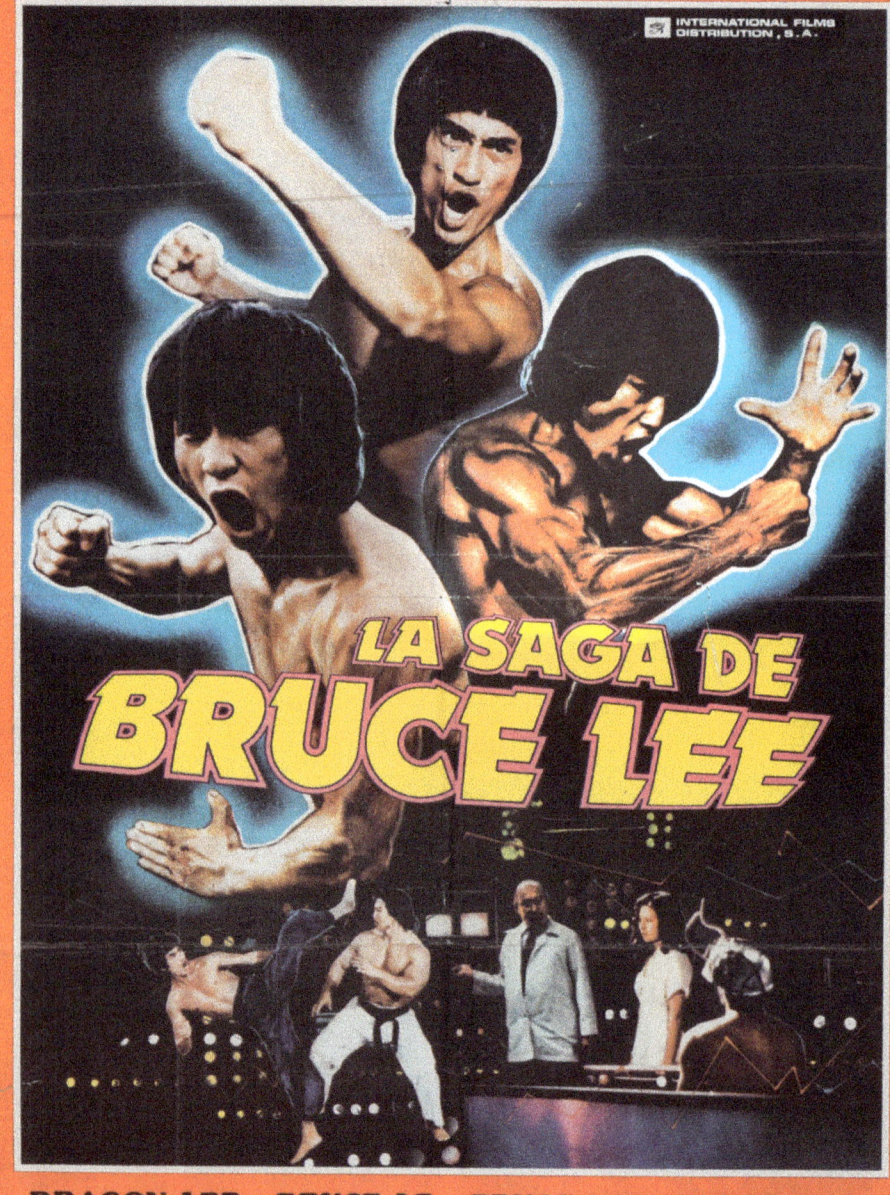

Spanish poster

Bruce Lai is a clone of Bruce Lee!

Pocket powerhouse Dragon Lee is soon wowing the filmmakers on set and gets a job, but western killers White Panther and Quick Tiger (Grand) are sent to kill Bruce 1 just in case, y'know, he's an agent. Bruce 1's battle with these two dudes is somewhat shambolic, though, probably due to the rather unimpressive on-screen fighting skills of the two western actors.

Bruce 1 is then informed that Chai Lo is preparing to dig up his gold soon (why does Chai Lo bury his smuggled gold, I wonder, does he think he's a pirate?), and in due course Bruce 1 beats up all the film crew baddies in a fight that starts in some hills and ends on a ship transporting the gold.

Meanwhile, Bruce 2 & 3 are briefed on their job, which will require them to travel to Thailand and eliminate a doctor processing narcotics there. The two clones meet their contact in Thailand, a dude named Charles (Chuck) Lee Singh, played by Bruce Thai, who looks just like a clone of Bruce Lee himself! Rather than dive straight into their mission, these guys do some sightseeing and head to the beach. Here a bunch of naked girls dance about, then start applying suntan lotion... and, I know, this isn't integral to the plot, but it adds to the fun, exploitative nature of the low budget production! All these naked girls chase a skinny guy along the beach and jump on him, so the Bruces head for their accommodation, where Bruce 3 discovers a nude girl waiting in his bed. This undressed babe tries to stab Bruce 3, but Bruce 2 chops her in the throat.

Bruce Thai looks like another Bruce Lee clone, but he isn't one!

Bruce Le fights Bolo!

Soon Bruce 2 & 3 and Chuck start combating the drug smuggling gang... and Bruce Thai fights with lots of Bruce Lee mannerisms, even though he isn't a clone. It really should be noted that Bruce Thai actually looks more like Bruce Lee than the three actors who are playing the clones of Bruce!

It turns out that the evil doctor has moved away from dealing in narcotics and is now dabbling with what seems to be a herbicide of some kind: we're shown some grass being turned brown and the doctor proclaims, "Soon I will conquer the whole world! Today we conquer Thailand, and ➡

These dudes look good in shades!

tomorrow the entire world!" But the Bruce clones have other ideas and attack the doc's scientists, with Bruce 2 pouring chemicals over one of them.

But we discover that the doctor has yet another bizarre plan when, at the villain's old wooden factory HQ, we watch as he experiments on victims, turning them into living bronzemen (say what?!) These metal-skinned killers are basically a bunch of guys in their underpants, spray-painted with gold paint. Cheesy coolness!

The doc decides he needs some downtime with his three naked female assistants, one of whom dances for him. With this cheesecake interlude dealt with, we're soon watching the Bruces fighting the bronzemen in what seems to be a quaint family garden, rather than at the factory, as the combatants battle near a kid's slide and a rotary clothes line, with a twee flower border seen in the background, running along the base of a neat wooden garden fence. The Bruce clones' fists ineffectually clang against the skin of the bronzemen, but then one of the steel-skinned dudes lands face-first on a bunch of poisonous leaves, which he, of course, decides to munch on... and he dies! Now our heroes, armed with handfuls of poison plants, go back into action! Stuffing what looks like grass in the bronzemen's mouths, the Bruces win the battle. Yay!

At this point Professor Lucas decides he isn't being appreciated by the SBI, goes rogue, and plans to use his control over the

A mad doctor's lab!

Stuffing poisonous leaves into the bronzemen's mouths!

The unhinged professor orders Bruce Lee 1 to fight Bruce Lee 2!

Bruce clones to prove he's a genius... but, rather than use all the clones to do his bidding, he decides to set them against each other so that he can find out which one is the best. Er, great plan, fella.

Bruce 1 and Bruce 3 are commanded to fight to the death, and Bruce 2 is ordered to attack 1 & 3! The clones clash for a while, until rebellious lab assistants release the clones from Lucas' control by cutting some wires - and now the Bruces are free to open a can of whoop-ass and rip into the professor's guards! There's a lot of fighting, including deadly skirmishes with Bolo and the other teachers, and a snake versus monkey style showdown between Bruce 2 and a pale-faced zombie guard (Cheng Kei-Ying), and finally the prof is arrested.

No doubt due to the availabilities of the different actors, resulting in the stars being shot at different times, the movie almost never has all the clones together on-screen, but is this really a big problem? This is a Bruceploitation yarn featuring buff Bruce lookalikes who're meant to be clones of him, and the movie is chock-full of action and interesting elements, like cheap 'n' cheerful lab sets, a corridor of 'death light' lasers, a large, beeping computer with primary-coloured light panels, plus some smatterings of nudity! Goofy, ridiculous and very watchable, *The Clones of Bruce Lee* boasts one of the all-time best, most memorable Bruceploitation movie titles ever!

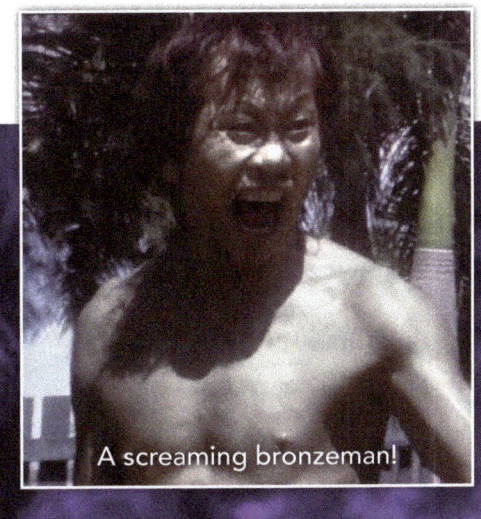

A screaming bronzeman!

THE DRAGON LIVES AGAIN (1977)

Starring Bruce Liang, Shen Ie-Lung, Tang Ching, Alexander Grand, Nick Cheung Lik, Eric Tsang, Lily Foo Lai, Jenny, Bobby Canavarro, Fang Yeh, Wong Mei, Cheung Hei, Yuen Siu-Tin
Written by Chi Lo, Liang Wei
Directed by Lo Chi
Produced by Hendrick Gozali
Goldig Film Company

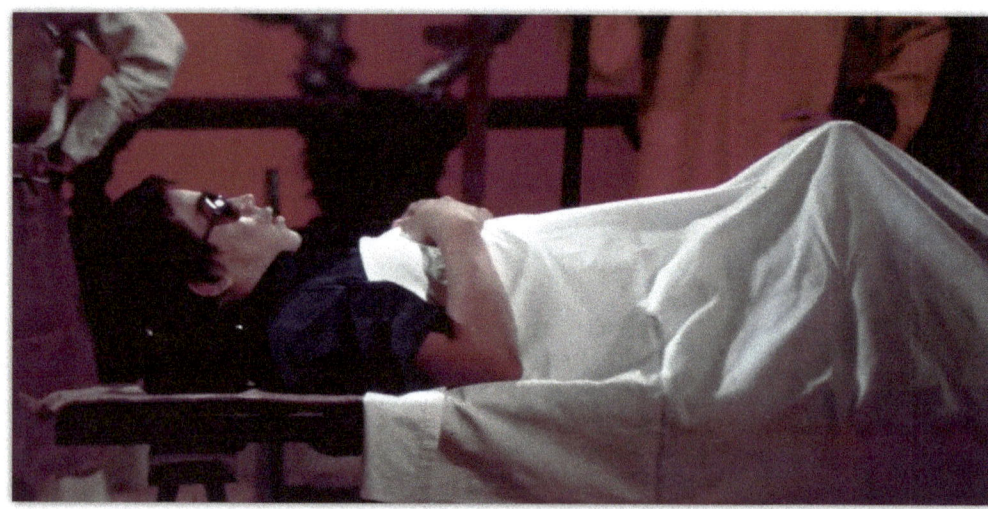

Bruce Lee dies and wakes up in the underworld, makes friends with some of the nicer folks there, including Popeye and the One-Armed Swordsman, and clashes with other characters, such as James Bond, the King of the Underworld, The Godfather, Clint Eastwood, Dracula and Zatoichi!

Aka *Deadly Hands of Kung Fu*, this is a movie that has to be seen to be believed!

After a caption that reads 'This film is dedicated to millions who love Bruce Lee', *Enter the Dragon* music kicks-in and then the Bond theme takes over, as James Bond faces-off against Bruce Lee! Awesomeness! This film is immensely enjoyable from the get-go, as characters we'll be meeting in the movie strut their stuff during the extended shot-against-red credit sequence.

We're then shown Bruce Lee's body lying in the cavern/throne room of the King of the Underworld (Ching)... and it looks as if Bruce died with a massive erection... but this impressive stiffness turns out to be his nunchucks! Lee is played by Bruce Liang (aka Bruce Leung) who, let's be brutally honest, is probably the Bruceploitation star who looked least like Bruce Lee, and the filmmakers obviously know this, so they have a character comment that, "It so happens when a person dies their face and their body undergo a change." This explanation must also be the reason why Clint Eastwood, Popeye and Dracula are all asian in this film!

Bruce soon comes to terms with the fact he's dead and that he's in hell, which pretty much resembles a Chinese town with a small casino and restaurants. There are also some cavern dwellings and a quarry. The underworld's residents defer to the King, mainly because he has the power to cause earthquakes by shaking a pillar,

though a shady cabal led by The Godfather have plans to take over the territory.

Bruce visits the main town restaurant and encounters Popeye (a youthful Eric Tsang), while elsewhere in the establishment Zatoichi the blind masseur/swordsman catches flies and puts them in his food, so that he can get out of paying his bill. Then Zatoichi, along with James Bond, Clint ➡

Eastwood (dressed as the Man With No Name), and a bunch of dudes in skeleton costumes confront Bruce in the restaurant, and Bruce starts to feel sweaty and dizzy, making it easy for Clint to beat him up. Fortunately for Bruce, he's cared for afterwards by Wa To (Siu-Tin), the doctor to the King of the Underworld, who's such a good doctor he even helps skeletons! Bruce admits during his convalescence that his Achilles heel when he was alive was that he played around too much and says aloud that he's sorry to Linda, his wife.

What makes this production so enjoyable

BRUCE LEE AS KATO

are all the famous characters added to the mix, with some of them depicting real-life people like Bruce Lee and Clint Eastwood and others representing fictional characters like Popeye, the One-Armed Swordsman, Zatoichi and Kwai Chang Caine from the *Kung Fu* television show. So it's great fun when the film cuts to Clint Eastwood, The Exorcist, Emmanuelle, Zatoichi and James Bond hanging out together in The Godfather's cavern HQ. There's no rhyme or reason to why some characters, like Bond and Emmanuelle, are played by western actors, and why Clint Eastwood, The Exorcist, etc, are played by asian actors. I guess we just have to remember that 'when a person dies their face and their body undergo a change', even when they're

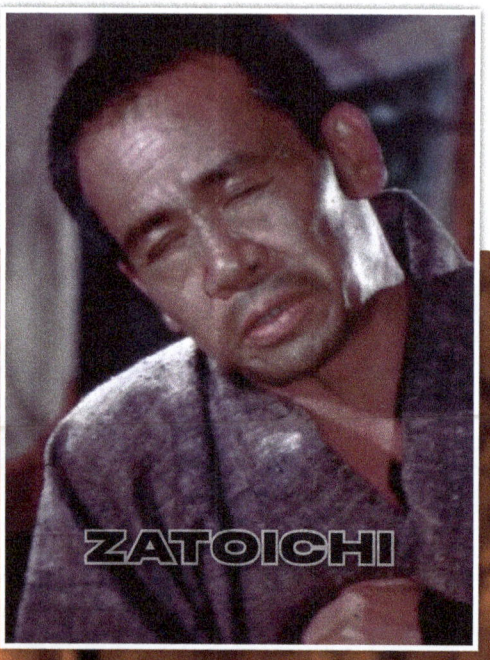
ZATOICHI

DRACULA

SKELETON DUDE

THE GODFATHER
THE EXORCIST

fictional characters like The Godfather!

Bruce does a little gambling at a casino, but he then tells everyone they should stop gambling because that is probably the reason they ended up in the underworld. He meets the One-Armed Swordsman here and strikes up a friendship with him.

We also get to see some of the naked underworld concubines in a large bath, chatting about Bruce Lee, discussing the Hollywood actors he trained, and musing about how they'd like to go out with him.

The movie jumps from obvious sets to obviously real-world locations without attempting to disguise the transitions, mainly when Bruce and other characters dash from the town studio set and end up immediately in a bright exterior quarry location. I think this editing just adds to the hey-we-don't-give-a-f**k-what-you-think mindset of the filmmakers!

At the quarry Bruce duels with Zatoichi, and each fighter takes turns to use different styles against the other, with the name of each technique superimposed on-screen. Zatoichi uses these styles: 'Blind Man Finds Way', 'Blind Chicken Peaks', 'Blind Man Kills Mosquito', 'Blind Snake Climbs', 'Blind Fool Massages' and 'Blind Dog Pisses'! Bruce, meanwhile, uses these special techniques, inspired by movie titles: 'The Big Boss', 'Enter the Dragon', 'Way of the Dragon', 'Fist of Fury' and 'Game of Death'!

For a while the movie shifts into sex farce territory, with the King of the Underworld cavorting and playing blind man's buff in

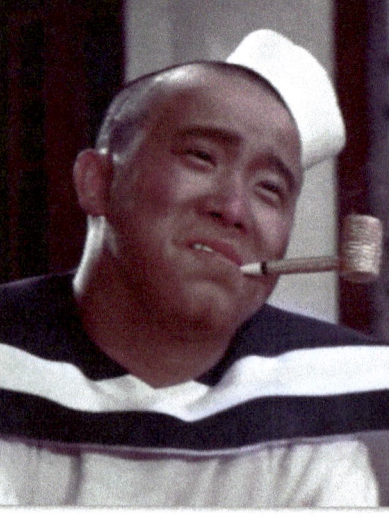

promises to become the King's wife.

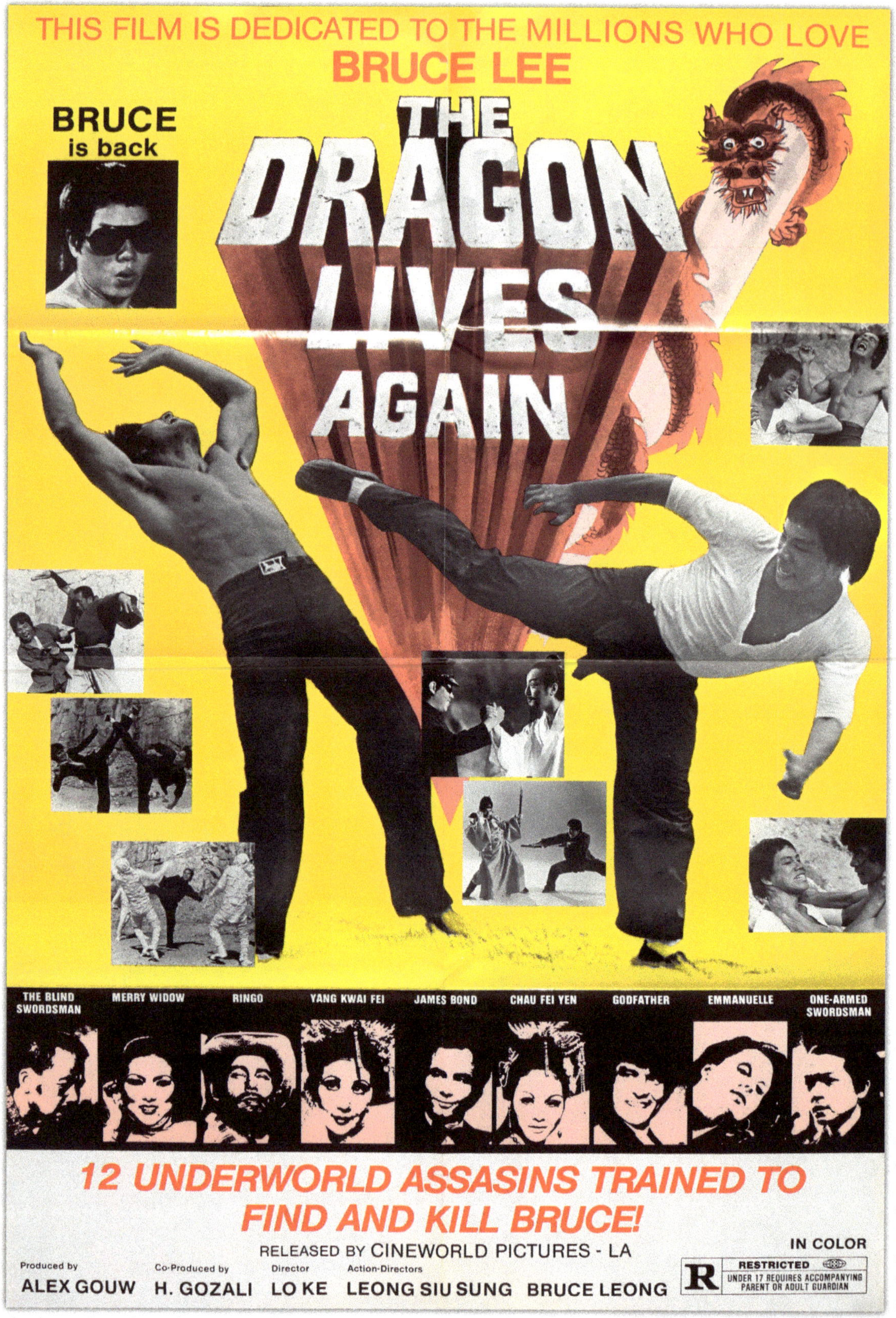

Dracula (Hei) shows up now with his skeleton henchmen (referred to as zombies) and Bruce arrives to take them all on dressed as Kato from *The Green Hornet!* Bruce gets pinned to the ground by the henchmen, who hold onto his arms and legs, so that Dracula can bend down, ready to bite him... and, suddenly, a third leg shoots up from Bruce's groin area, booting Dracula in the face, as an on-screen title informs us this style is called 'The Third Leg of Bruce'! Insane stuff!

Back with Emmanuelle and the King, they have sex in his pink-lit bed. There's lots of moaning and groaning and Bruce has to intervene to warn the King that Emmanuelle was trying to give him a heart attack through pleasure, and the King muses that, "Her pussy's in this plot too, she was using it to murder me."

Bruce is made the new captain of the King's bodyguards, triggering reprisals from The Godfather's team, resulting in Bruce killing James Bond and then Clint Eastwood. The Exorcist and The Godfather decide to try and kill the King, who defends himself by creating an earthquake by shaking the

the hot tub with nude women, for no particular reason, plot-wise, other than to show off some attractive nekkid ladies. We also get one of the underworld concubines and the Queen of the Underworld planning to seduce Bruce, which involves them trying to give him a potion to 'stiffen his resolve'. The foxy Queen even tells Bruce, "Beat me hard with that terrible weapon"! The concubine and the Queen end up forcing each other to drink the potion, however, and they both become scabby-faced hags. Meanwhile, sexpot Emmanuelle meets-up with the King of the Underworld. "You can spank my botty," she informs him, and she

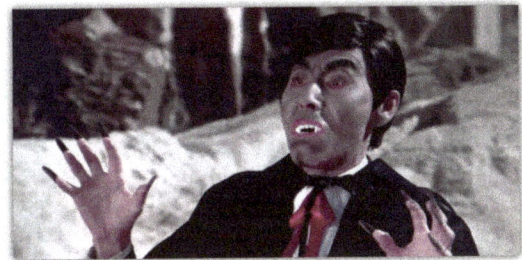

pillar, so they then decide to attack Bruce. This fight between Bruce, The Exorcist and The Godfather is very nicely done, in fact it's thrilling and totally ace, as Bruce finishes off The Godfather (played by a very cool-looking Shen Ie-Lung) by utilising his 'Fingers of Fury' technique!

Knowing that Bruce is angry with him for causing an earthquake that hurt innocent people, the King implores General Cheung Fei to help him rid himself of Lee... so Cheung Fei leads a mob of bandaged mummies to attack Bruce! Popeye, the One-Armed Swordsman and Kwai Chang Caine come to Bruce's aid and a madcap final martial arts skirmish takes place in the underworld quarry. Popeye gets kicked about... so he eats a can of spinach and the 'I'm Popeye the Sailor Man' tune plays as he beats-up the mummies! The One-Armed Swordsman slashes the mummies with his sword and Bruce battles General Cheung Fei with nunchucks! This is excellent stuff, with Bruce finally being granted permission to leave the underworld.

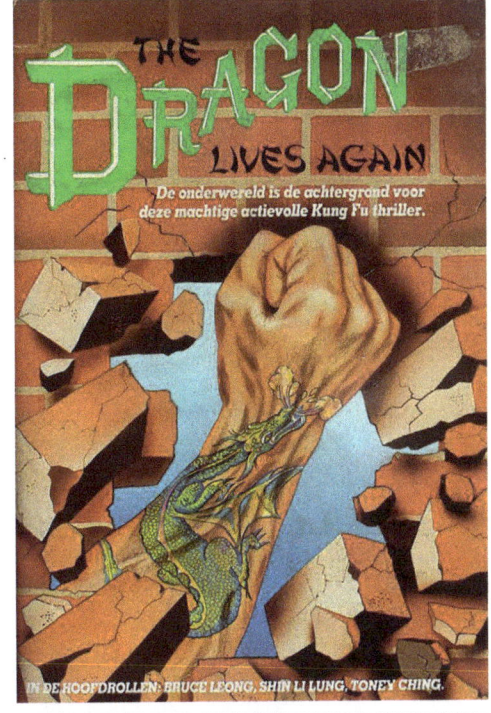

Dutch VHS cover

Bruce uses *Enter The Dragon* style!

The Dragon Lives Again is a priceless, peculiar pantomime of preposterous proportions. The movie would have been a stand-out Bruceploitation flick solely because of its totally unhinged storyline, but what makes it even better, what provides the exciting icing on the crazy cake, is the fact that the action is really, really good. Bruce Liang may not resemble Bruce Lee, but he looks really bloody good on-screen in the many fight scenes that were choreographed by him.

ENTER THE CLONES OF BRUCE (2023)

Starring Bruce Li, Bruce Le, Dragon Lee, Bruce Liang, Eric Tsang, Godfrey Ho, David Chiang
Directed by David Gregory
Produced by Andrew Furtado, Michael Worth, Jeremy Kai Ping Chueng, Vivian Sau Man Wong, Frank Djeng, Carl Daft, David Gregory
Severin Films

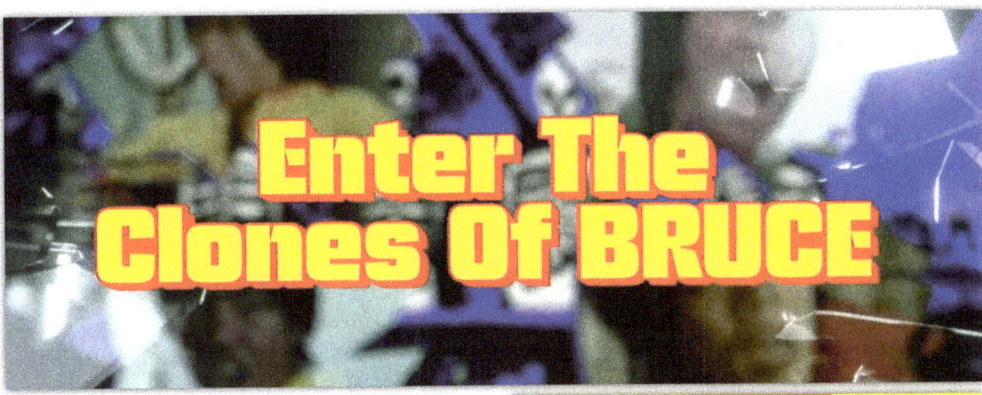

This feature-length documentary plunges into the very wild and exciting world of the Bruceploitation genre and brings us along for the riotous, rollicking ride! Director David Gregory, who made the immensely entertaining documentary *Lost Soul: The Doomed Journey of Richard Stanley's Island of Dr. Moreau* (2014), uses the very start of the film to set the scene, detailing Bruce Lee's rise to stardom and then the shock that was felt following Bruce's untimely death in 1973. International audiences were left wanting more Bruce Lee movies, so producers eagerly fed the need by supplying films of all kinds linked somehow to Bruce Lee. Some of these productions were biopics that were less than accurate depictions of his life, others were the continuations of stories told in earlier Bruce Lee films, some focused on characters meant to be related to the characters Bruce played previously, others had protagonists investigating Bruce's death, and all manner of other ploys were utilised to somehow link the films to the late martial arts legend, including editing footage from Bruce's childhood films into the story, using shots from Bruce's actual funeral, or, sometimes, just adding 'Bruce' to the movie's title.

Some distributors simply lied and claimed that Bruce Lee was actually the star of their flicks! Key to the viability of this sub-genre was the use of Bruce Lee lookalikes, and these actors - these clones of Bruce Lee - are the main focus of this documentary.

Enter the Clones of Bruce is jam-packed with film clips and heaps of interviews, comprising of chats with Bruce clone actors, like Bruce Li and Bruce Le, and other actors and commenters too, including Eric Tsang, Godfrey Ho, Yasuaki Kurata, Michael Worth, Ron Van Clief, Roy Horan, Phillip Ko, Casanova Wong, Angela Mao, Andre Morgan, Joseph Lai and Lo Meng.

The doc details how the Bruceploitation movies were made by a lot of independent companies, who very often aimed their releases at the western market. These films starred asian leads thanks to the fact Bruce Lee had disrupted the film market by becoming a superstar, helping to promote and validate the idea that asian actors were just as capable of portraying characters that were tough, charismatic and sexy.

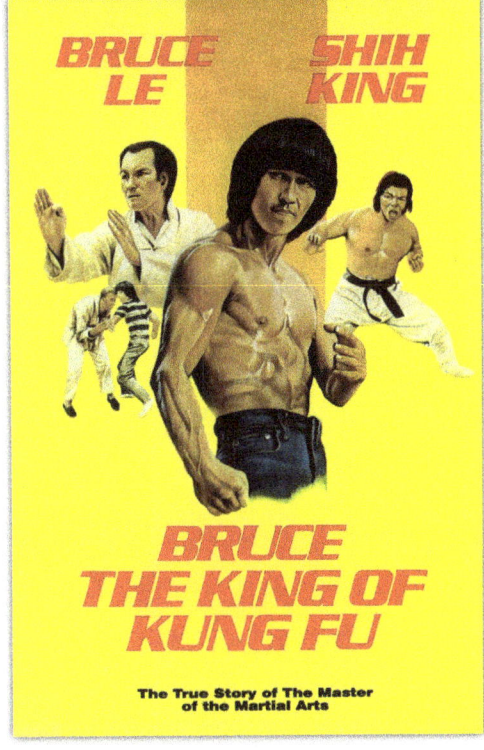

David Gregory covers a great deal of different, interesting details and facts. He highlights how France helped to drive the kung fu market, and how German distributors flagrantly called the lead actors in these Bruceploitation films 'Bruce Lee' even if, in reality, the

Bruce Li being interviewed for the documentary (above)
Bruce Li from one of the many film clips used in the doc (right)

Casanova Wong

The utter, total legend that is Godfrey Ho provides his thoughts and insights

movies is, of course, looked at, as is the tendency of the Bruceploitation films to become increasingly absurd and strange. Such bizarre titles that are name-checked include *Bruce Lee Against Supermen*, *Bruce Lee Fights Back From the Grave*, *The Dragon Lives Again* and *The Clones of Bruce Lee*, which was one of the insane pinnacles of the sub-genre, with its tale of a professor creating multiple Bruce Lee clones easily seen as a metaphor for the whole Bruceploitation phenomenon. The sub-sub-genre of *Game of Death* rip-off movies is looked at, revealing how the images from the unfinished, unreleased Bruce Lee movie (publicity shots of Bruce wearing the iconic jumpsuit and Bruce fighting various opponents in a tower, etc) inspired filmmakers to make their own versions of the story, with Bruce clones in jumpsuits climbing up pagodas and battling exotic foes. Then, when Golden Harvest finally released *Game of Death* in 1978, it was obvious that Bruce Lee lookalikes and stand-ins had been used to expand the production to feature-length, helping to make this film come across as simply a very lavish, very well publicised Bruceploitation picture! *Game of Death*, let's remember, uses footage from Lee's actual funeral and (gasp) features the legendary, infamous scene that attempts to pass someone off as Bruce by sticking a cutout photo of Bruce Lee's face to a mirror!

actors involved were actually Bruce Li or Bruce Le. The Germans would justify this approach by claiming that 'Bruce Lee' was a synonym for great martial arts fighting!

The incorporation of footage from Bruce Lee's funeral into various Bruceploitation

The key clone actors interviewed are Bruce Li, Bruce Le, Dragon Lee and Bruce Liang, and they all offer interesting

In the documentary actor Yasuaki Kurata reveals that he didn't even know that he'd been renamed 'Bruce Lo' in the US prints of *The Tigers Claw*!

Producer Joseph Lai

The great Bruce Le is interviewed and the documentary features loads of clips from his movies

anecdotes and insights. Bruce Li reveals that he was actually uncomfortable playing Bruce Lee, even saying that it repulsed him. But he adds that he didn't have a choice as this was where he could find work (he once worked for a whole week with no sleep). Li admits that he went through a rough time once he had a family, trying to provide for them, and says that he found new purpose once he started studying osteopathic medicine. Dragon Lee confesses that he was not that particularly fond of being a Bruce Lee impersonator either, though he does acknowledge that doing all the Bruceploitation productions did enable him to make a lot of movies.

Enter the Clones of Bruce touches upon the fact that, funnily enough, Sammo Hung, who definitely doesn't physically resemble Bruce Lee, is rated as the best Bruce Lee imitator, with his *Enter the Fat Dragon* proving to be an entertaining, funny, respectful piss-take of the Bruceploitation sub-genre.

The documentary benefits from articulate insights from Michael Worth, who is one of the film's producers, and it adds extra zip to the proceedings by including some cool, eye-catching motion graphics (courtesy of Kyle Broom) and uses the fun, funky, fantabulous song 'King of Kung Fu', by Kandy, as its theme tune, so *Enter the Clones of Bruce* certainly begins with a bodacious bang!

Towards the end of the doc there's some reflection on the fact that the glory days of Hong Kong & Taiwanese kung fu film

The Clones of Bruce Lee (1980)

production are definitely long gone, with the filmmakers visiting some dilapidated former film studios, but *Enter the Clones of Bruce* ends on a positive note, with the clone actors showing that they still like to practice their kung fu moves!

This is a very enjoyable documentary that will keep viewers who're unaware of the whole Bruceploitation sub-genre just as entertained as the die-hard fans.

EXIT THE DRAGON, ENTER THE TIGER (1976)

Starring Bruce Li, Chang Yi, Lung Fei, Chin Kang
Written by Chang Hsin-Yi
Directed by Lee Tso-Nam
Produced by Wang Feng

Bruce Lee asks his friend Tiger to be his successor should anything happen to him, so when Lee does die suddenly Tiger makes it his mission to discover the true facts behind the action icon's demise.

Bruce Li plays Bruce Lee at the start of this flick and he also portrays the Tiger, so there's Bruce Li x 2 on the screen for a while when the two dudes are chatting with each other! This movie is guilty of using real footage from Bruce Lee's funeral (like so many other Bruceploitation films also did), then the plot kicks-in, focusing on Tiger travelling from Singapore to Hong Kong, where he becomes embroiled in the machinations of a gang that had been trying to blackmail Bruce Lee to smuggle drugs for them. Central to the gang's blackmail plan was Susie, the woman who was with Bruce when he died. It transpires that Susie has a tape proving that Bruce was being blackmailed, so everyone wants to get their paws on this evidence.

Various scenes are set in places that have Bruce Lee posters taped to the walls, as if the characters in this movie need to keep Bruce's memory alive, even if it's just via a cheap poster stuck to the garish 70's-style wallpaper. This maybe subconscious yearning extends to Tiger, who obviously resembles Bruce, so he's often mistaken for the dead star by gangsters and even by patrons at a go-go bar.

Also known as *Bruce Lee: The Star of Stars*, this film has lots of fights located in rundown industrial buildings and grubby scrapyards. People get kidnapped and beaten up frequently in the story, and Tiger dons some disguises, pretending to be a bearded newspaper seller and then a telephone repairman.

Similar in some ways to Li's *Bruce Lee, We Miss You!* (1975), this movie is better shot than that film, and it ends with a showdown on an atmospheric, craggy shoreline, where two damsels in distress are tethered to large rocks as Tiger battles the arch villain, known as The Baron, and his duo of red sweater-wearing goons. Here The Baron assails Tiger with a sword stick, so the barechested, bloodied Tiger uses the crashing waves to his advantage, finally defeating his foe. This ending looks pretty amazing, it's really great stuff, and is far better than the rest of the movie!

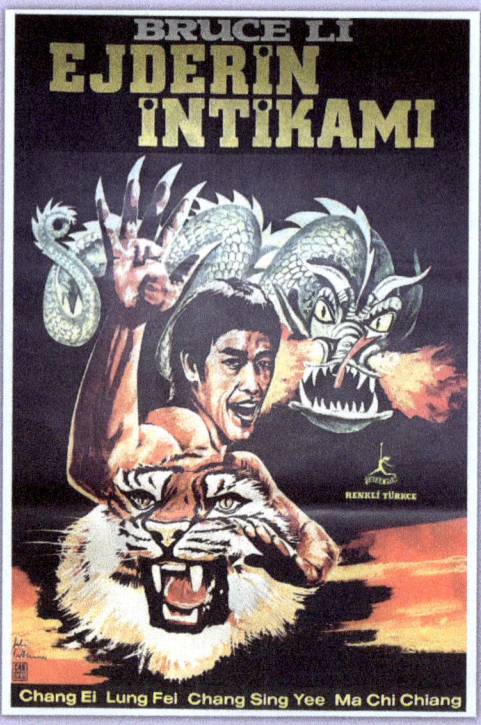
Turkish poster

Totally awesome French poster for Exit the Dragon, Enter the Tiger (1976)

In the realm of martial arts cinema, few names carry as much weight as Bruce Lee's. His impact on the genre is seismic, immeasurable, inspiring countless filmmakers and performers to emulate his style and charisma. One such figure who flirted with the Bruce Lee impersonation scene, but with his own unique twist, was none other than Sammo Hung, a unique, super-talented martial artist, actor, and filmmaker in his own right.

Through movies like *Enter the Fat Dragon* and *Skinny Tiger and Fatty Dragon*, Sammo Hung paid homage to Bruce Lee while carving out his own niche in the martial arts comedy genre.

The Early Years

Sammo Hung's journey into the world of martial arts and cinema was deeply rooted in his upbringing in Hong Kong. Born into a family entrenched in the local film industry, Hung's parents worked as wardrobe artists, leaving him under the guardianship of his grandparents. Notably, his grandmother was the archetypal martial arts actress Chin Tsi-Ang, while his grandfather was the esteemed film director Hung Chung-Ho.

At the young age of 9, Hung embarked on a pivotal chapter in his life when he joined the China Drama Academy, a renowned Peking Opera School in Hong Kong. It was a decision influenced by his grandparents, who learned about the school from their acquaintances. Under the tutelage of Master Yu Jim-Yuen, Hung spent seven formative years honing his skills. Adopting his sifu's given name as his family name, Sammo Hung became known as Yuen-Lung. His time at the academy was marked by his membership in the prestigious Seven Little Fortunes performing group, where he fostered a friendly rivalry with a fellow student, Yuen Lou, who later rose to fame as Jackie Chan.

Hung's early exposure to the film industry came at the age of 14 when he was handpicked by a teacher with connections to perform stunts in a movie. This experience ignited his passion for filmmaking, particularly in the intricacies of camera operation. Despite his budding career, Hung remained deeply connected to his peers, often sharing his earnings with his opera school brothers.

However, a setback struck just before his departure from the academy when he was 16 years old. An injury confined him to bed for an extended period, during which his weight significantly increased. Undeterred, Hung found his footing in the film industry

German Blu-ray cover (the title translates as *The Little Fat Man with the Super Punch*)

Sammo Hung, of course, appeared in both *Enter the Dragon* and *Game of Death*

as a stuntman, earning himself the moniker "Sam-mo", derived from a popular Chinese cartoon character known for its distinct three hairs.

In this manner, Sammo Hung's early years laid the foundation for his illustrious career in martial arts cinema, marked by his dedication, resilience, and an unwavering passion for the craft. Sammo Hung developed a friendship with Bruce Lee, with Hung serving as Lee's sparring partner in the opening scenes of Enter the Dragon. This early exposure to Bruce's work left an indelible mark on Hung, influencing his approach to martial arts cinema.

Enter the Fat Dragon

In 1978 Sammo Hung directed Enter the Fat Dragon, a film that would cement his status as a martial arts comedy icon. Drawing inspiration from Bruce Lee's classic Enter the Dragon, Hung put his own spin on the martial arts genre by infusing it with humour and lots of exaggerated action sequences.

The premise of Enter the Fat Dragon revolves around a rotund martial artist named Lung, played by Hung, who must navigate a series of comedic misadventures while uncovering a criminal conspiracy. Through his portrayal of Lung, Hung pays homage to Bruce Lee's iconic characters while injecting his own comedic flair into the mix. One of the movie's most memorable scenes sees Hung spoofing Bruce Lee's famous nunchaku fight, albeit with a comically oversized pair of chopsticks. It's a testament to Hung's talent and wit that he's able to simultaneously honour Lee's legacy while poking fun at the tropes of martial arts cinema.

Skinny Tiger, Fatty Dragon

Sammo Hung continued to explore the intersection of martial arts and comedy with films like Encounters of the Spooky Kind (1980) and Winners & Sinners (1983), and in 1990 he starred in Lau Kar-Wing's Skinny Tiger and Fatty Dragon. This time, he teamed-up with frequent collaborator Karl Maka to deliver a rollicking buddy cop comedy that pays homage to Bruce Lee's Way of the Dragon, when he goes fist to fat with Mark Houghton. Other set pieces paid homage to the classic Hong Kong action films of the 1970s. Hung and Maka, playing the mismatched police officers, must put aside their differences to take down a notorious crime syndicate and, along the way, they find themselves embroiled in a series of hilarious situations that showcased Hung's mastery of physical comedy and martial arts choreography.

Sammo Hung is the G.O.A.T, like Bruce!

Sammo Hung's contributions to the martial arts comedy genre cannot be overstated.

Through films like Enter the Fat Dragon and Skinny Tiger and Fatty Dragon he not only paid tribute to Bruce Lee but also carved out a distinct identity for himself as a top filmmaker and performer. Hung's influence extends far beyond his own filmography, inspiring generations of film professionals and martial artists to explore the comedic potential of the genre. His ability to blend action and humour with heart and authenticity has earned him a lasting legacy in the annals of Hong Kong cinema. Interestingly, Donnie Yen embarked on his own reinvention of Enter the Fat Dragon (2020) when he took on the challenge of portraying a rotund martial artist, very reminiscent of Hung's iconic role. Just as Sammo Hung paid tribute to Bruce Lee in his own distinctive way, Donnie Yen's homage serves as a testament to the enduring legacy of one of Hong Kong cinema's most influential figures. ●

Skinny Tiger and Fatty Dragon (1990)

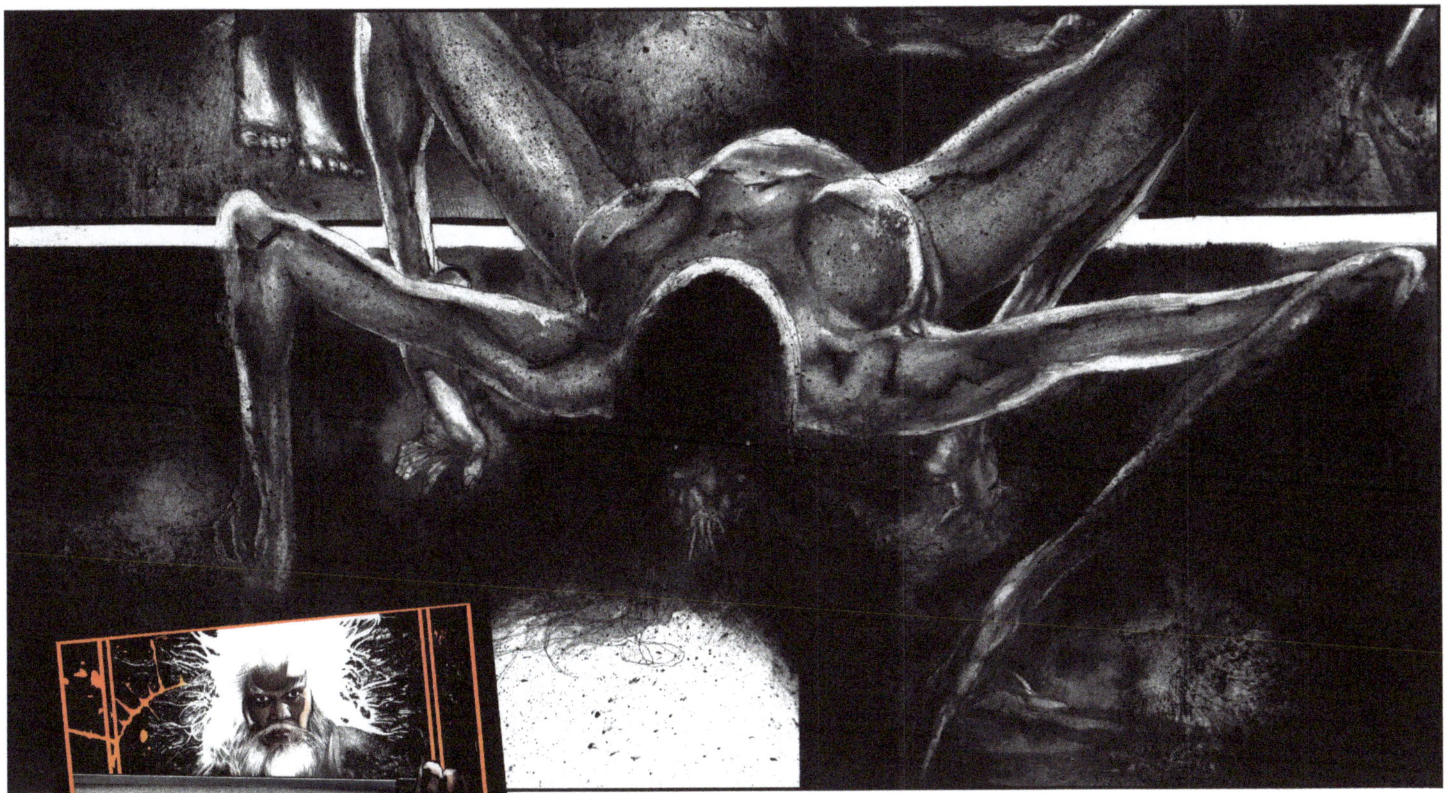

RUSSELL FOX

COVER ARTIST FOR *FILM FRENZY* ISSUE 2 AND THE COMIC SERIES *VAMPIRELLA VS PURGATURI.* ILLUSTRATOR ON *JUDGE DREDD, A WITCH,* AND MORE!

TO COMMISSION STORYBOARDS + ILLUSTRATIONS, AND SEE MORE OF HIS WORK, VISIT:

LONEFOXANDCUB.COM

Born in Brooklyn, New York City, **Ron Van Clief** joined the U.S. Marines, did boot camp in Camp Lejeune, was stationed in Okinawa, in Cuba, and in the Philippines, and saw active duty in Vietnam. His military decorations include the Rifle Sharpshooter Badge, Marine Corps Good Conduct Medal and National Defense Service Medal.

After his military service Ron became a New York City Transit Police Officer from 1965 to 1968. He was a Senior Defensive Tactics Instructor for the US Secret Service too.

Ron studied various martial arts styles with masters Moses Powell, Peter Urban and Frank Ruiz, and he co-founded the Chinese Goju system.

Ron became a movie star after he snagged a five picture deal, which kicked off with Yangtze Productions' *The Black Dragon* (1974). Some of Ron's movies include *Bamboo Trap* (1975), *The Super Weapon* (1976), and *Way of the Black Dragon* (1978), plus some Bruceploitation productions: *Kung Fu Fever* (1979), the utterly odd *Fist of Fear, Touch of Death* (1980), and the ace *The Black Dragon's Revenge*, aka *The Death of Bruce Lee* (1975).

Ron was the martial arts choreographer on *The Last Dragon* (1985), which starred Taimak Guarriello, who was one of his students. Recently Ron featured in the new documentary *Enter the Clones of Bruce* (2023).

Ron is a 5-time world karate/kung fu champ & a 15-time all-American champion. He has competed in both full-contact and non-contact karate tournaments in New York and several other national tournaments.

Ron has also written a number of books, including *The Manual of the Martial Arts, Black Heroes of the Martial Arts,* and *The Hanged Man: The Story of Ron Van Clief.*

Ron was inducted into the International Sports Hall of Fame by Arnold Schwarzenegger and Dr. Robert Goldman.

And, as if all this wasn't enough for one man...

...Ron was given his nickname 'The Black Dragon' by the legendary Bruce Lee!

When did you get into martial arts? Back then there was no Bruce Lee explosion, so what was the reason you became interested?

I was into gymnastics, this was 1958, and I walked into the St. John's Community Center and I saw Moses Powell, rolling out on a hard wood basketball floor. He didn't make a sound. So smooth. It was amazing, and then he did a self defence demonstration where he took on like eight people. Wow. And that inspired me. I was hooked and then, when I went downstairs, there was Ronald Duncan, also teaching martial arts. So I studied with both of them until I went into the Marine Corps. When I travelled overseas, posted at different places as a soldier, to Okinawa in Japan, to Hong Kong and the Philippines, I would study martial arts there.

And you've remained interested in martial arts to this day?

Yes, I started Brazilian jiu-jitsu in 2011 when I was 68 years old, and I still do it three nights a week.

Ron and Bruce!

How did you meet Bruce Lee?

I was fighting at a tournament in New York, the All-American Championship.

German artwork for *The Black Dragon* uses an image of Bruce Lee!

Ron (billed here as Ron Van Cliff) liked working with Carter Wong

WAY OF THE BLACK DRAGON

CECILIA WONG HANG SAU
CARTER WONG RON VAN CLIFF
CHARLES BONET JIM PATTERSON

CHAN LAU HO FAT KWONG PAK SA LIT SALLY NEWARAJ
ROBERT BLACKWOOD ROSE RAPHAEL

AN YEO BAN YEE'S PRODUCTION FREDDIE YIN CHAN CHO

CHAN CHO EDDIE WANG TITUS HO SERAFIM KARALEXIS CHAN WUI NGAI

have the spirit - you're the Black Dragon." I've had that nickname ever since.

Being called the Black Dragon is already cool, obviously, but the fact that the name was given to you by Bruce Lee is just the coolest icing on the cake!

Yeah, it was so cool.

Was this the era when Bruce was doing The Green Hornet?

Yes. I'd never met him before. Anyway, we went back to the hotel he was staying at, which was right by Madison Square Garden. He was a cool guy. We stayed up for hours talking philosophically and smoking weed and, you know, just chilling. He was an interesting guy.

At what stage did you think of getting into movies?

I was a model with the Black Beauty Model Agency and my agent was called Betty Forray, who was a big time agent. She called me and said, "I got a gig in Hong Kong. Five movies. Go to the audition." I went to the audition and producer Serafim Karalexis picked me, and a month later I wound up in Hong Kong working on *The Black Dragon*.

I got to Hong Kong and they shipped me directly to the Philippines where, in like six weeks, they shot the first Black Dragon film.

I did a bunch of films, in Thailand, in Korea, in the Philippines.

I loved working with Carter Wong. A really cool guy, I mean a really cool guy. He was a serious martial artist. We sparred in the hotel and he gave me a black eye one day! He was like a really cool guy.

Bruce was in the audience, he was like in the first row and I was fighting for the Grand Championship. I fought this gentleman by the name of Joe Hayes. He was a truly amazing athlete, a pro boxer, and his kicks were a thousand percent better than mine. He beat me by two points. Bruce came up and I took a picture of Joe standing with Bruce, and Bruce said, "You know, you're the Black Dragon." I said that I just lost the bout, but Bruce said that it didn't mean anything. He said, "You

Charles Bonet and Ron in *The Black Dragon's Revenge*

Bamboo Trap (1975), aka The Black Panther of Shaolin

Were there any differences in how the films were shot in the different countries?

Shooting in Hong Kong and shooting in the Philippines were two different methodologies. The Chinese had a small crew. The Filipinos had a larger crew, and people were running all over each other, you know? With the Chinese, everybody on that crew could do every job.

These films were all shot quickly?

We shot the second Black Dragon film, *The Death of Bruce Lee*, in three weeks, man. That's it.

I love that film.

It's great. But it was filmed in three weeks. It was crazy.

Were you jumping from one film to the next?

Yeah, I went to the Philippines. Then I went to Thailand to shoot the film *Way of the Black Dragon*.

***Way of the Black Dragon* is quite a weird, hybrid production, because the first 30 minutes or so is an exploitation film about some Thai women being trafficked and being used as drug mules, but then, suddenly, you appear and the movie becomes an action film!**

I know, it was like, wow. Yeah. I had a contract to do five films, and you don't really have a say in the quality or the theme or the essence of the films.

How about the fight choreography? Did you have any influence with that?

The first one, no.
But in the second one I was one of the main choreographers. And the third and the fourth and the fifth.

How was it on the set of *The Death of Bruce Lee*, aka *The Black Dragon's Revenge*?

Charles Bonet and I used to smoke a lot of weed on the set, you know. And Jason Piao Pai, one of the stunt coordinators, was one of my good friends.

You've got good chemistry with Charles Bonet in that film

Yeah. Charles passed away a few years ago.

He was really good in *The Death of Bruce Lee*. Do you have a favourite co-star from the films you were in?

It'll always be Carter Wong for me. We had a really good time in Thailand. I mean, I trained with him when I was there. I learned three section staff from him. And butterfly knives. He was really a character. Tough as nails, man. His fists were like iron.

I mean, the only other person who was like that, that I had met, was Leo Fong, who almost knocked me out in the hotel one night when we were filming a movie called *Bamboo Trap*. We were sparring, and he punched, and... bang. I was unconscious, man.

Way of the Black Dragon (1978)

Were you surprised about the percentage of actors that didn't know martial arts in the Hong Kong films? Because some were actors pretending to know martial arts, whereas you were, of course, a real martial artist.

You know, I met the guy that did *Five Fingers of Death*, Lo Lieh: he was an actor. He knew nothing about kung fu.

Was there a language barrier when you worked on these films?

On my initial shoot, I felt a little isolated. No one spoke English, except my assistant. I was in a barracks kind of sleeping situation, with the crew, the cast, everybody staying in the same place, you know. And nobody spoke English. The guy that helped me, he only came the days that we were actually on the set. So, have you ever seen the film *The 13th Warrior*, with Antonio Banderas? In that film he became totally immersed in that country, in that area, and learned the language from listening. That's what happened to me. A month went by, and, to me, I actually heard English coming from these guys when they were speaking, no kidding.

The Black Dragon's Revenge (1975)

At the time did you go to the cinema to see any of the films you'd been in?

I saw two of the films that I did in the movie theatres, one in the Philippines and one in Hong Kong. I saw *The Black Dragon's Revenge* - aka *Death of Bruce Lee* - in Hong Kong when it opened. I was surprised how many people came to see it. I mean, it was like, it was kind of amazing, you know.

There was a hunger, after Bruce Lee died, to see anything that was somehow linked to him - and then there was a bit of a backlash from Lee fans at the time, when they felt misled by much of the advertising.

Oh my goodness, the production company of *The Death of Bruce Lee* was taken to court, so they changed the title to *The Black Dragon's Revenge*.

A photo from Bruce Lee's funeral, showing a close-up of his face in the coffin, was on that poster.

Yeah, I know.

But that photo was removed, thankfully. The poster looked great without it, because it was illustrated by the awesome Neal Adams. It must've been very cool to be drawn by Neal Adams.

He was a good friend of mine. I watched him draw.

What are your thoughts on Bruceploitation? Because on the one hand, obviously, it can be seen sometimes as a cash-in on the name

This version of the poster doesn't feature the photo of Bruce Lee in his coffin

Film Frenzy   Page 92

of Bruce Lee, but looked at another way, it functioned as a reminder of how much Bruce Lee was missed.

I think that many of these Bruceploitation films paid homage to Bruce. And I think that it was important that his memory was embedded in the minds of people, which these films to a certain extent helped to do, so that people could carry his legacy forward. Because he was a genius, not just a nice guy. He would talk at length about the psychology and physiology of martial arts. He was way ahead of his time. He was including boxing, grappling, wrestling, dancing, all kinds of stuff in his repertoire.

In the feature-length documentary *The Super Weapon* (1976) your technique is nicely showcased, but also, as Bruce Lee also did, you share your insights too, you're not some guy that just wants to fight: you've got thoughts behind it all. *The Super Weapon* really showcased your skills well, so would something like that have helped gain more public interest in your classes and your techniques?

Oh, of course.

Actually, some months ago, I spoke to Serafim Karalexis about doing *The Super Weapon 2*, which would feature some of the people from the original film that are still alive.

That'd be great. Are the other guys still in good shape, as fit as you?

Most are not. I understand that it can be hard to stay fit - I go through lazy times myself, but I try to make myself go to the dojo or the gym every day. I say, "Get your fat fuckin' ass on that bus and get to the dojo", because I know that, once I get there, everything is going to be great. It's just the getting there sometimes. But I go there, get in some rounds, all the drills, all the self defence. It's great. I'll leave exhausted and beat up because everybody's 50 or 60 years younger than me! I've never seen anybody my age on the mat actually sparring. I've seen them teaching, doing seminars, but I've never seen anyone my age on the mat.

Everyone else there must give you a lot of respect for that, though.

I get that a lot from the young guys. They say, "How old are you? Holy shit!"

I did transfer from the hard style of karate and kung fu to jiu-jitsu. It was easier on my body. I competed in 900 tournaments in over 55 years of competition. Imagine that? 55 years. I took a lot of punches and kicks and teeth knocked out, jaw broken, ribs broken, all kinds of stuff. But, in jiu-jitsu, you don't have those kinds of injuries. You have strains, pulls, your back would go out, or your knee, or something like that, but no repetitive concussions.

I don't know anybody from my era, still alive, that's in the kind of shape that

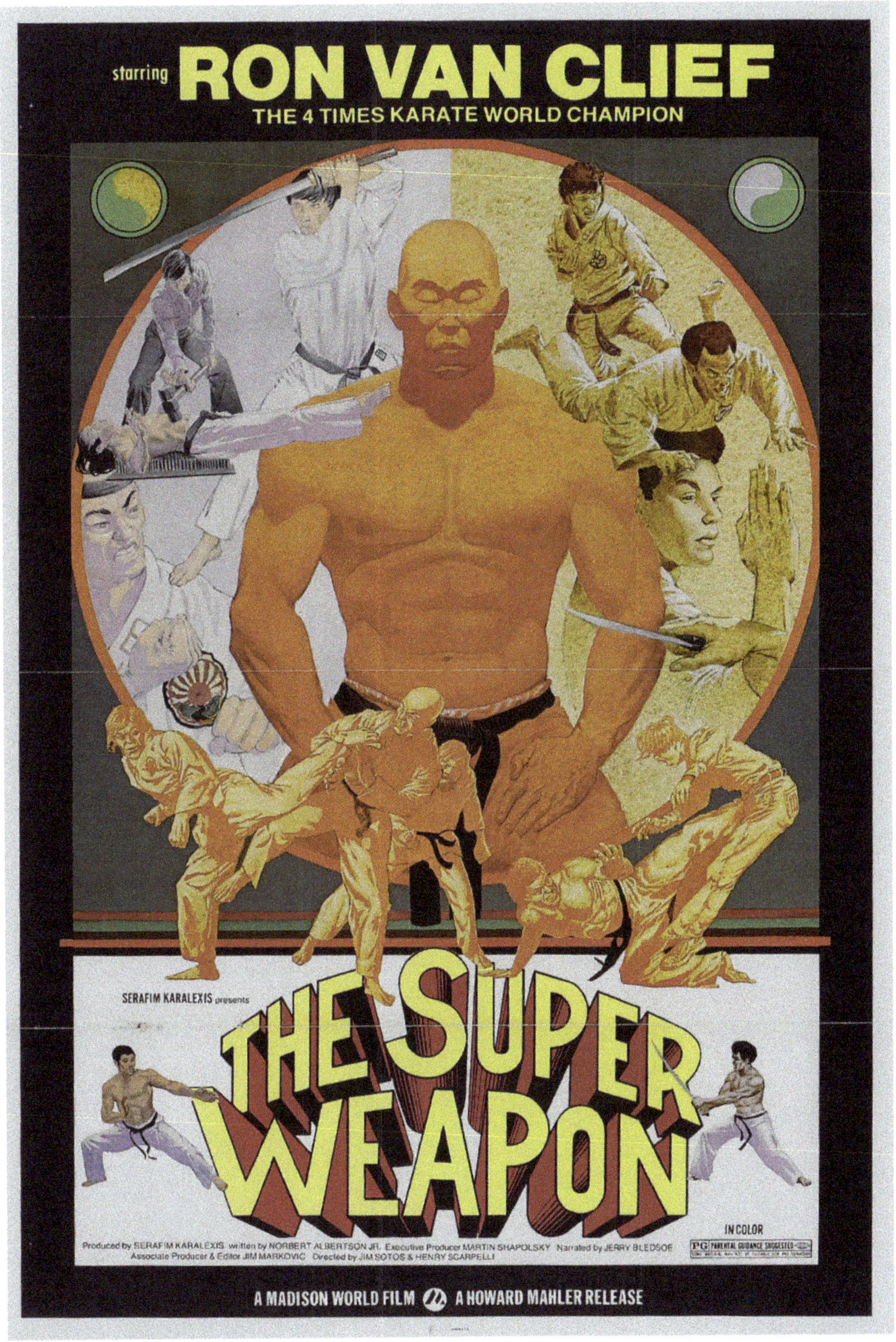

It doesn't matter what age Ron is, you don't mess with him, okay?

I'm in. I ran the marathon two years ago here in Hawaii.

I see that there's a project called *Tao of the Black Dragon*, which features a character who is, of course, completely based on you as you were back in the day, at your virile peak!

It's a 90-minute animated film. It's going to be in 3D. I've got a 'Black Dragon Mobile', which is a Lamborghini that flies and goes under the water. I've got jet packs, so I can jump and fly like Superman. I mean, it's like unbelievable. I have to do the voiceovers for it.

Ron as a 3D cartoon character!

I've played the beta demo of a *Tao of the Black Dragon* video game online. Is this made by the same people doing the animated film?

Yeah. My character's going to be fighting in a pagoda, like Bruce did in *Game of Death*. I'm a co-producer on this project, both for the game and the film. It's going to be really good. This James Bond-type character that I'm playing, at one point, goes in a time machine, and you not only see a young Ron Van Clief Black Dragon, you also see an older guy training agents, and that's also me: the older Black Dragon in the future.

Well let's hope the project gets finished, it sounds and looks awesome!

The animation is amazing. It's truly amazing.

You are in a movie called *Hot Lead Hard Fury* (2018), which was filmed on Super 8 to make it resemble a low budget, grungy Grindhouse-style film. They really went retro on that one.

I really enjoyed working on that. They did shoot that on Super 8 to make it look like a Grindhouse movie. I had a lot of fun working on it.

Now let's talk about a film called *Fist*

Ron pilots a speedboat in the demo game!

of Fear, Touch of Death* (1980), which is a fake documentary. They filmed a lot of it at Madison Square Garden during the 'Oriental World of Self Defence' event, but the filmmakers pretended it was actually the '1979 World Karate Championships'. They included lots of old footage of Bruce Lee, who was dubbed saying stuff he never really said. This film is like the opposite of *The Super Weapon*, in that *Super Weapon* was a well done, factual documentary, whereas this is mainly fake. There's a sequence where you are interviewed as you're hitting a punch bag. Did you have any idea what the whole film would be like?*

I had no idea. Producer Terry Levene called me and said he had some work for me. I said, "Of course, Terry." I went down and did what he asked me to do and that was it. Fred Williamson is the highlight.

He's funny in it, sending himself up good-naturedly when he has to deal with different folks mistaking him for Harry Belafonte!

Fred's a great guy. He's 86 years old now.

Ron, you're the real deal. You were a martial arts world champion multiple times. You were a U.S. Marine. You fought in Vietnam. You were awarded the Sharpshooter Badge amongst other medals. You were a New York cop. You were an instructor for the US Secret Service.

I trained Secret Service agents for 20 years.
Thousands of agents.

Do you think your various life experiences helped you when you were making movies? You did cool stuff that other actors only pretended to do, but you did it all in real life.

It probably did help me, all those experiences. But I'm of the now.

Forget about the past and the future, I always live in the now.

I don't think about the future, really. I know now, as an old fart, that I don't have as much time left as I've already lived. But I will make it to a hundred.

My mother passed away a few years ago at the age of 97. My mother was a track runner, she went to an all-girls school and she was a track star, so even into her 80s and 90s she'd walk ten blocks, twenty blocks.

Do you think you get your genes from her, for your health and longevity?

Yes. She was the toughest woman I've ever met.

You were in *The Squeeze* (1978), a New York-set Italian/German heist movie, where you played a bad guy called Duke. The movie starred Lee Van Cleef. I liked the fact that there was a Van Cleef and a Van Clief in this film and I was hoping you two would have a confrontation: Van Cleef versus Van Clief! But you exit the movie when one of the lead characters, played by Edward Albert, stabs you in the back with a metal hook, so you don't have a face-off with Lee.

We didn't do any scenes together, that's correct, but I met Lee Van Cleef at least ten times on the set. He was a really nice man. We were talking about the old days, the old westerns, like *High Noon* (1952).

Even in *The Squeeze* he's first seen as a rancher, wearing a stetson.

Yeah. He was a really nice man and Karen Black, who was also in the film, was a really nice lady.

Did you mind playing villains? You're a villain in *The Squeeze* and you're a bad guy in *Kung Fu Fever* (1979).

It didn't matter to me. The experience of being on the set and actually working with an ensemble was wonderful. The part really didn't matter. Lots of times I didn't like the character, or the dialogue. But, you know, you're hired to do a gig, and it's good to play a range of characters, because range is important, and I did so many films in Hong Kong as a bad guy. With wigs, with beards, with moustaches. Crazy, huh?

Your facial hair was magnificently cool in the 70s: you sported different manly moustaches, an afro, big sideburns.

I was a bit of a black hippy for a while, took LSD, went to Woodstock. Those were the days, man.

You've had a full life, Ron.

No regrets, no regrets. It's been a good life.

And a part of that life involved making Bruceploitation films. Thanks in part to the internet, and people like Michael Worth and David Gregory, there's a real reevaluation of the Bruceploitation genre taking place now.

That's wild.

Gone are the days when some people were offended by Bruce Lee's name and image being used by movies to make a buck. Now viewers can just

Big, bad Ron vs Dragon Lee!

watch these films and be entertained by them.

People can enjoy the action and, hopefully, sometimes the Bruce Lee spirit comes off the screen.

These films can, at the very least, give folks another reason to think about Bruce Lee again. As exploitative as some of the Bruceploitation films are, they endure because of Bruce Lee's impact on action cinema. Without him they obviously wouldn't exist.

I don't really consider most of these to be exploitation films. They're just an extension of his legacy.

Ron is interviewed in *Enter The Clones of Bruce* (2023)

The name 'Bruceploitation' was attached to the sub-genre early on and it stuck. It is, admittedly, a pretty cool name!

Even the last actual Bruce Lee film, *Game of Death*, was a Bruceploitation movie. They put a photograph of Bruce's face on a mirror, to hide the stand-in actor's face.

Has anybody, any viewer, ever been fooled by that 'mirror face' effect?! But, regardless of that and all the Bruce Lee proxy actors used in *Game of Death*, I do still enjoy the film.

Yeah, me too.

What are you doing after this interview?

I take an afternoon BJJ (Brazilian jiu-jitsu) class. I take two night classes also. I'm thinking of testing for black belt in the next two years.

Your commitment to martial arts is amazing. Some people go through phases of being interested in martial arts, but you're still doing it and striving to get better and better.

Training for me is fulfilling my passion. I've always been workout-mad.

It's really been great chatting with you, Ron.

It's my honour, guys. Thank you so very much for this.

I'm a bit in awe of you, actually!

Hey, I'm just Ron (laughs). ●

BRUCEPLOITATION
POSTER GALLERY

A COOL RANGE OF EYE-CATCHING POSTER ARTWORKS SHARED BY DAVID GREGORY & MICHAEL WORTH

Words: Ken Miller

An integral part of the Bruceploitation sub-genre was the need for cool, colourful posters to help cinemas, and especially grindhouses, sell their products to prospective patrons. These posters varied in quality, from well-painted illustrations to slapped-together photo montages. A lot of these artworks featured the great Bruce Lee himself as the hero of the posters, even if Bruce Lee DIDN'T appear in the movies they were promoting! And many of these movie posters, such as *Bruce Lee Fights Back from the Grave*, were definitely guilty of promising more than the films themselves could ever hope to deliver!

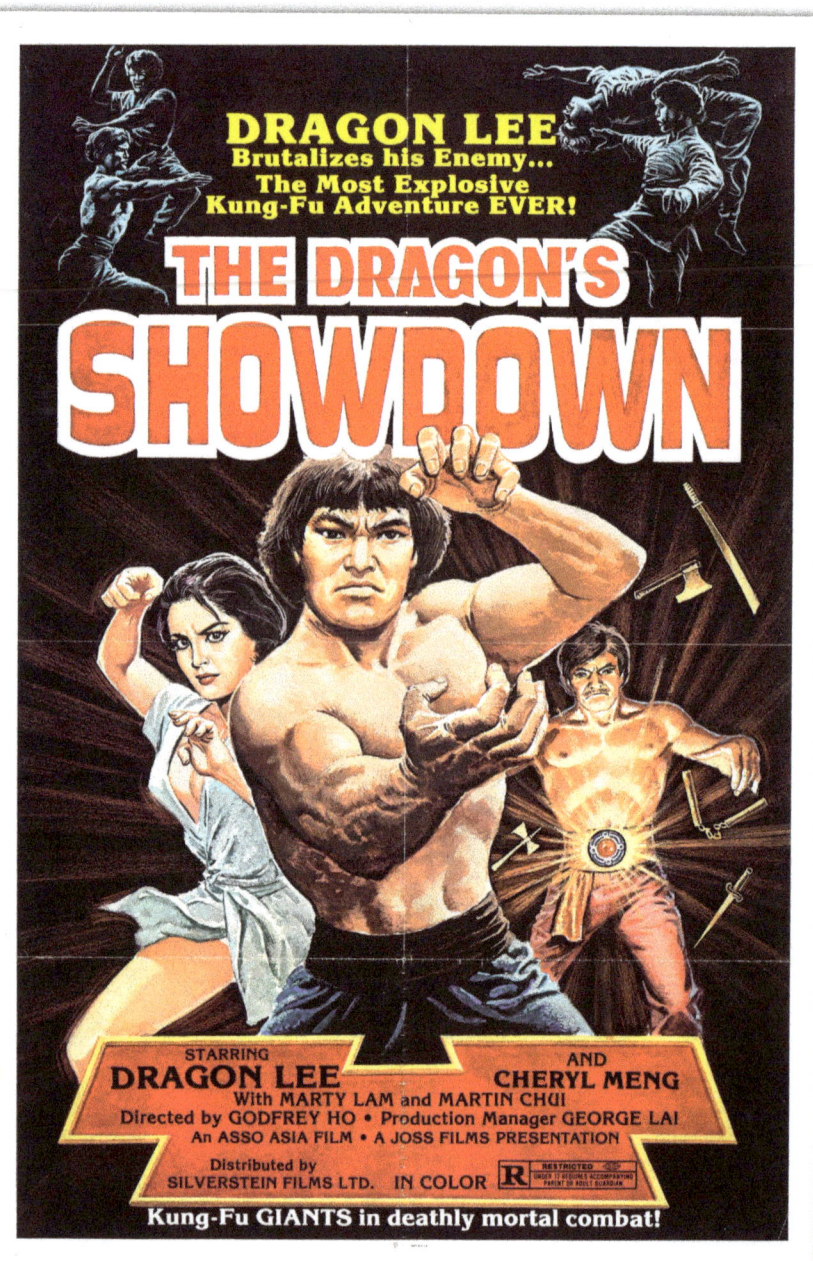

The Dragon's Showdown (1980) Also known by the equally Bruceploitation-esque title *The Dragon's Infernal Showdown*, this Asso Asia Films production sees Dragon Lee learning kung fu from a drunken master.

Enter the Game of Death (1978) This Thai poster obviously likes to show star Bruce Le multiple times, and why not, eh?

Bruce Lee Fights Back from the Grave (1976) Wow, what an outrageous poster and film title! The bat-creature here is basically a rip-off of the bat seen on the cover of Meat Loaf's album 'Bat Out of Hell'... but with a guy's head added! Ace!

Fist of Fury Part Two (1977) I love the pulpy style of the poster painting for this Bruce Li movie, also known as Fist of Fury II and Chinese Connection 2.

Call Me Dragon (1975) Ouch! "Super action like you've never seen before!" The subject matter of this very impactful US poster's illustration is, well, literally eye-popping!

The Deadly Silver Ninja (1981) Regardless of the actual merits of the film, which is known by several other titles, including *Dragoneer 8 - The Unbeatable*, this poster illustration is stonkingly awesome!

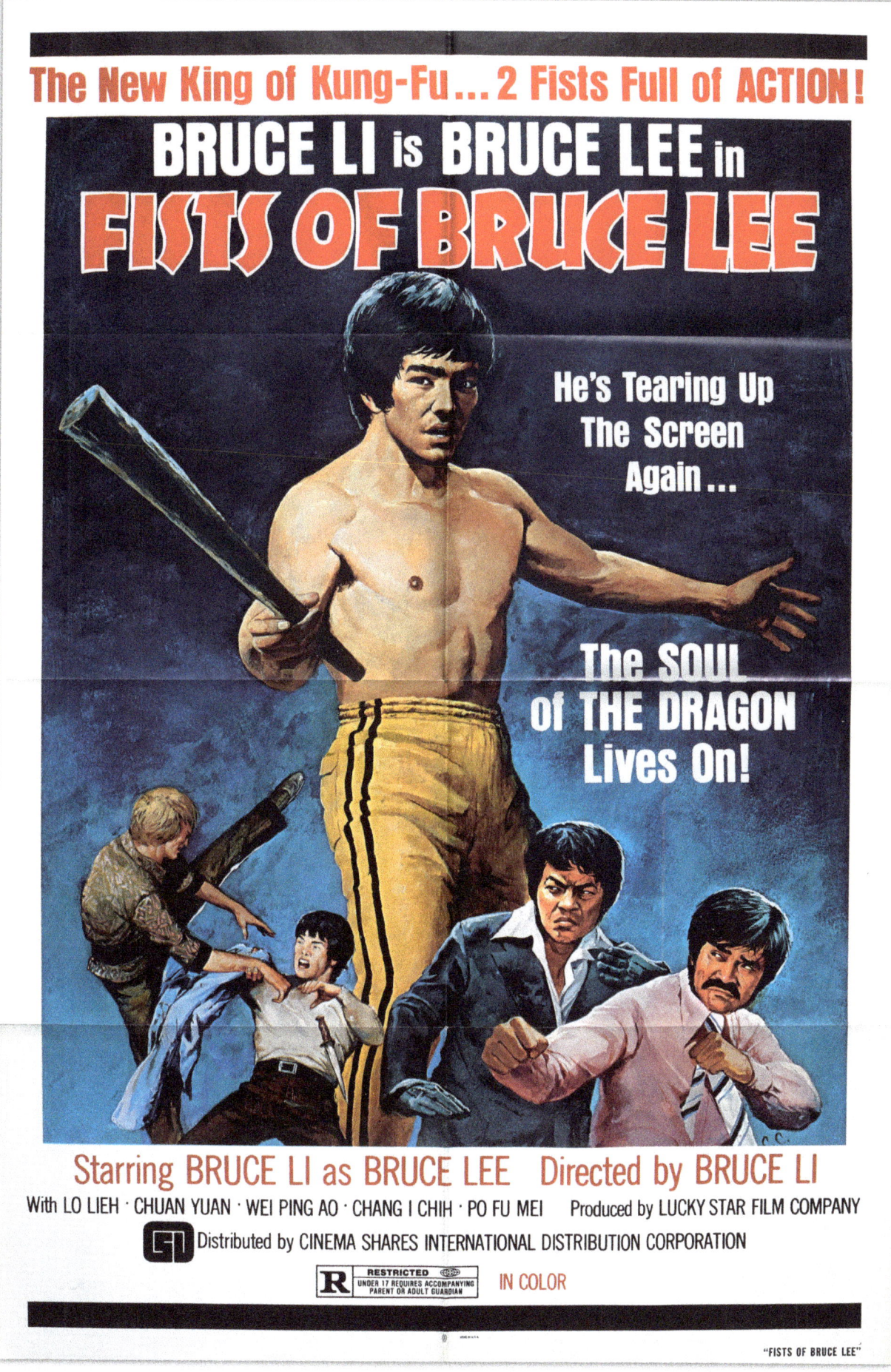

Fists of Bruce Lee (1978) Here's a poster with another solid illustration. Maybe the artist didn't manage to capture Bruce Li's likeness here, though I'm sure the brief was to make the hero look a bit like Bruce Lee…

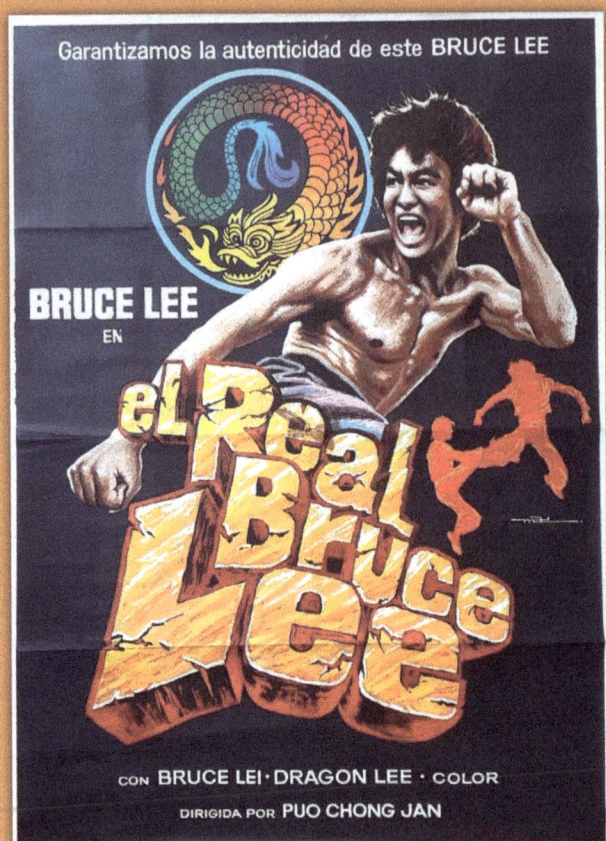

The Real Bruce Lee (1977) A cool Spanish poster!

Enter the Game of Death (1978) Here's an Italian poster that features a wonderful painting of Bruce Lee, rather than Bruce Le!

Bruce Lee, We Miss You! (1975) This Australian poster doesn't bother to credit or show Bruce Li, the actor that plays a martial artist who, because he is so upset Bruce Lee has passed away, decides to go on a mission to discover what really happened to his idol... and he is aided on this quest by the spirit of Bruce Lee himself (also played by Bruce Li)! The above poster decided to focus on an image of the actual Bruce Lee (like so many other Bruceploitation posters did)... and, for good measure, it also includes a gravestone with Bruce Lee's name written on it!

***Exit the Dragon, Enter the Tiger* (1976)** Finally, here's a poster that does brilliantly capture Bruce Li's likeness. This is a nicely-painted illustration! Though the image of Bruce Lee in his coffin is in questionable taste, it is lovingly-painted.

www.ingramcontent.com/pod-product-compliance
Lightning Source LLC
Chambersburg PA
CBHW061125170426
43209CB00013B/1669